Christian Philosophy

ETIENNE GILSON

Translated by Armand Maurer

This little book puts into English Etienne Gilson's *Introduction à la philosophie chrétienne*. Almost lost among his more voluminous writings, it is nevertheless significant for its expression of his more mature views on Christian philosophy.

First formulated as a way of philosophizing under the influence of Christian faith, in later years Gilson broadened and deepened the notion by also tying it closely to theology. This development in the concept of Christian philosophy was a consequence of his discovery of the true nature of medieval theology, especially in the works of Thomas Aquinas – a discovery that he documents in his autobiographical *The Philosopher and Theology*.

In ten brief chapters Gilson illustrates the concept of Christian philosophy with central themes in the metaphysics of Thomas Aquinas, including the notions of being and essence, their real composition in finite beings, cause, substance, participation, the divine ideas, and God as pure Being. These and other metaphysical doctrines are shown to emerge within faith and theology and under their direction and guidance. Gilson throughout emphasizes the deeply spiritual aspect of this metaphysics. Its appeal, he insists, is not only to the mind but to Christian piety and love.

THE ETIENNE GILSON SERIES 17

Christian Philosophy
An Introduction

ETIENNE GILSON

Translated by Armand Maurer

Pontifical Institute
of Mediaeval Studies

CANADIAN CATALOGUING IN PUBLICATION DATA

Gilson, Étienne, 1884–1978.
  Christian Philosophy : an introduction

(The Etienne Gilson series, ISSN 0708–319X ; 17)
Translation of: Introduction à la philosophie chrétienne.
Includes bibliographical references and index.
ISBN 0–88844–717–5

1. Philosophy and religion. 2. Ontology. I. Maurer, Armand A.
(Armand Augustine), 1915– . II. Pontifical Institute of Mediaeval Studies. III. Title. IV. Series.

BL51.G513 1993   200'.1   C93–095183–2

Printed by
HIGNELL PRINTING LIMITED
WINNIPEG, MANITOBA, CANADA

*The translation is dedicated to
the Christian philosophers*

JOSEPH OWENS, CSsR
and
HENRY B. VEATCH

Contents

Translator's Introduction

Throughout Etienne Gilson's long career as an historian of philosophy and a philosopher in his own right, one of his main concerns was the validity of the notion of Christian philosophy.[1] As early as 1924 he applied the notion to the philosophy of St. Bonaventure, and again in 1929 he used it as an apt description of St. Augustine's philosophy.[2] Rumblings of dissent could be heard in reviews of these books, and at conferences in Paris in 1931 and in Juvisy in 1933 some of the leading lights of French philosophy mounted an attack on the concept of Christian philosophy as a contradiction in terms and an illegitimate mixing of reason and

---

1. Besides the works of Gilson cited in the notes to the text, readers may also wish to consult the following for the notion of Christian philosophy: Jacques Maritain, *An Essay on Christian Philosophy*, trans. Edward H. Flannery (New York: Philosophical Library, 1955); Maurice Nédoncelle, *Is There a Christian Philosophy?* trans. Illtyd Trethowan (New York: Hawthorn Books, 1960); Joseph Owens, *Towards a Christian Philosophy*, Studies in Philosophy and the History of Philosophy 21 (Washington, DC: The Catholic University of America Press, 1990), pp. 1–173; Anton Pegis, *The Middle Ages and Philosophy* (Chicago: Regnery, 1963); John F. Wippel, *Metaphysical Themes in Thomas Aquinas*, Studies in Philosophy and the History of Philosophy 10 (Washington, DC: The Catholic University of America Press, 1984), pp. 1–33; *Christliche Philosophie im katholischen Denken des 19. und 20. Jahrhunderts*, ed. Emerich Coreth et al., 3 vols. (Graz: Styria, 1987–1990); and *Christian Philosophy*, a special issue of *The Monist* 75.3 (July 1992), ed. Joseph Owens.

2. Etienne Gilson, *La philosophie de saint Bonaventure* (Paris: Vrin, 1924), trans. Illtyd Trethowan and F.J. Sheed as *The Philosophy of St. Bonaventure* (New York: Sheed & Ward, 1938); *Introduction à l'étude de saint Augustin* (Paris: Vrin, 1929), trans. Lawrence E. Lynch as *The Christian Philosophy of St. Augustine* (New York: Random House, 1960).

faith, philosophy and theology.[3] In these debates Gilson, with Jacques Maritain and others, vigorously defended the validity of the term; and in his Gifford lectures in 1931–1932, later published as *The Spirit of Mediaeval Philosophy*,[4] he took up the subject from an historical point of view, showing that Christian philosophy is not an empty or contradictory notion but an historical reality. In this work he offers what is perhaps his first description of Christian philosophy. It is, he writes, "*every philosophy which, although keeping the two orders* [of philosophy and supernatural revelation] *formally distinct, nevertheless considers the Christian revelation as an indispensable auxiliary to reason.*"[5]

In later books and articles Gilson often returned to the theme of Christian philosophy, replying to critics, refining the notion, and developing its relation to faith and theology. *Christianisme et philosophie* appeared in 1936.[6] An important article entitled "What Is Christian Philosophy?" was published in 1957.[7] In 1960 Gilson devoted a chapter to Christian philosophy in his autobiographical *Le philosophe et la théologie*.[8] In the same year Gilson published two other books on Christian philosophy: *Elements of Christian Philosophy* (henceforth *Elements*),[9] and *Introduction à la philosophie*

---

3. See *Bulletin de la Société française de philosophie* [Paris] 31 (1931) and *La philosophie chrétienne*, proceedings of a conference held on 11 September 1933 at Juvisy, published in *Journées d'études de la Société thomiste* 2 (1933).

4. *L'esprit de la philosophie médiévale*, 2 vols. (Paris: Vrin 1932), trans. A.H.C. Downes as *The Spirit of Mediaeval Philosophy* (New York: Scribners, 1936; repr. Notre Dame, Ind.: University of Notre Dame Press, 1991).

5. *The Spirit of Mediaeval Philosophy*, p. 37, italics in the original.

6. *Christianisme et philosophie* (Paris: Vrin, 1936), trans. Ralph MacDonald as *Christianity and Philosophy* (New York, London: Sheed & Ward, for the Institute of Mediaeval Studies, 1939).

7. "What Is Christian Philosophy?" in *A Gilson Reader*, ed. A.C. Pegis (Garden City, New York: Hanover House, 1957), pp. 177–191.

8. *Le philosophe et la théologie* (Paris: Fayard, 1960), trans. Cécile Gilson as *The Philosopher and Theology* (New York: Random House, 1962).

9. *Elements of Christian Philosophy* (Garden City, New York: Doubleday, 1960).

chrétienne (henceforth *Christian Philosophy*),[10] which is translated
here for the first time. Though related in their subject matter, the
two books are not the same. Gilson wrote the *Elements* at the suggestion of Anton Pegis, his friend and colleague at the Toronto
Institute of Mediaeval Studies, who was then Director of the
Catholic Textbook Division of Doubleday & Company. There is no
French version of this work. About the same time Gilson wrote
the *Introduction à la philosophie chrétienne*. In a letter to Pegis in
1959, he describes it, with a touch of humor, as "your own *Elements* in tabloids. [It is] not, however, an abridgment, but rather
a succession of short chapters, each of which is a sort of meditation on some particular problem. The substance is the same
(where the subject is the same) but the approach is different.
There are no proofs of God's existence, no study of the transcendentals. My first idea was to write a sort of introduction to
Thomistic spirituality, some 'theological exercises' or 'theological
meditations.'"[11]

Gilson was pleased with his *Christian Philosophy*, for he refers
to it in the Preface of the final edition of his *Le thomisme*, commenting on its unusual style and its linking of metaphysics with
spirituality: "it is," he says, "a book written in a quite free-flowing
style. In regard to it I should like to think that others besides
myself will see there the tendency – should we call it natural or
supernatural? – of metaphysical speculation to be united to spirituality."[12]

In the final chapter of *Christian Philosophy* Gilson explains the
purpose and scope of the book:

10. *Introduction à la philosophie chrétienne* (Paris: Vrin, 1960).

11. Etienne Gilson to Anton Pegis, letter dated 31 August 1959:
Pontifical Institute of Mediaeval Studies collection, Archives of the University of St. Michael's College, Toronto.

12. *Le thomisme: Introduction à la philosophie de saint Thomas d'Aquin*,
6th ed. (Paris: Vrin, 1965), p. 8. Laurence K. Shook translated the fifth
French edition (published in 1948) with the title *The Christian Philosophy
of St. Thomas Aquinas*, with a catalogue of St. Thomas' works by I.T.
Eschmann (New York: Random House, 1956).

These thoughts [Gilson writes] represent neither the theology of St. Thomas Aquinas nor his metaphysics, even less all the conclusions he held as true in the area of the philosophy of nature. We have said nothing here about the human person, nothing about ethics or politics. But it was not our intention to speak of them. Our only wish was to elucidate as clearly as possible a small number of literally capital truths that must be grasped if the rest of the [Thomistic] doctrine is to be understood.

All these truths depend on a certain notion of being, which was that of St. Thomas, and without which there is no Thomism truly worthy of the name. It is on this notion that we wanted to center attention. We have tried to clarify it by showing how certain other notions, like those of substance or cause, which are rightly accounted metaphysical principles, are tied up with it.[13]

Gilson did not entirely abandon his original idea of offering his readers theological meditations and introducing them to Thomistic spirituality. The theological orientation of Christian philosophy is one of the most striking – and controversial – features of the book; but more about that later. Each of the ten chapters of *Christian Philosophy* is a meditation on a central theme of metaphysics, whose sole purpose is to bring the reader, as it did the writer, closer to the knowledge and love of God. To the critics who complain that Thomistic theology is harmful to Christianity because it neglects love, piety, and spirituality, Gilson replies that this is a complete misunderstanding of Thomism. St. Thomas's thought, he insists, nourishes the affective as well as the intellectual needs of the human person. Indeed, "far from excluding spirituality, [it] is in fact a spirituality."[14]

13. Below, pp. 132–133.
14. Below, p. 4; see also Gilson's lecture *Théologie et histoire de la spiritualité* (Paris: Vrin, 1943); and Walter Principe's *Thomas Aquinas' Spirituality*, The Etienne Gilson Lecture 1984 (Toronto: Pontifical Institute of Mediaeval Studies, 1984) and his "Affectivity and the Heart in the Theological Spirituality of Thomas Aquinas," *Spiritualities of the Heart*, ed. Annice Callahan (New York: Paulist Press, 1990), pp. 45–63.

The opening sentences of the Preface set the stage for the ten meditations that follow. Gilson understands by Christian philosophy the way of philosophizing described by Pope Leo XIII in his encyclical *Aeterni Patris*, and he takes as its model the one specifically recommended by Leo: Thomas Aquinas.[15] It is significant that the pope did not reduce Christian philosophy to a doctrine, not even that of Thomas Aquinas. Rather, he called it a way or method of philosophizing that has been used by Christians throughout the history of the Church. Those who follow this method, the pope says, unite to the study of philosophy obedience to the Christian faith. They philosophize "in the best possible way; for the splendor of the divine truths, received into the mind, helps the understanding, and not only detracts in no wise from its dignity, but adds greatly to its nobility, keenness, and stability."[16]

This is the sense in which Gilson understands Christian philosophy. As a method of philosophizing, it does not have an essence or nature, like philosophy itself or theology. These are two formally or essentially distinct wisdoms, each definable in terms of its own principles and methods. Christian philosophy does not add to them a third wisdom with an essence of its own – a sort of hybrid that would combine and, in the process confuse, faith and reason. Critics who accuse Gilson of creating such a hybrid notion (*une pensée bâtarde*, in his words),[17] fail to see that

15. For the text of *Aeterni Patris* see *Acta Apostolicae Sedis* 12 (1878–1879), pp. 97–115. Gilson edited an English translation of the encyclical in *The Church Speaks to the Modern World: The Social Teachings of Leo XIII* (Garden City, New York: Doubleday, 1954), pp. 31–54.

16. *Aeterni Patris*, ed. Gilson, p. 52. See Gilson, "What Is Christian Philosophy?" p. 186.

17. Below, p. 64 and n11. Fernand Van Steenberghen, to whom Gilson here refers, has recently reaffirmed his opposition to the notion of Christian philosophy; however, he asserts that he always taught that "the revealed truths, received by faith, enrich the Christian philosopher; they help him to produce an excellent philosophy ("les vérités révélées, reçues par la foi, sont enrichissantes pour le philosophe chrétien; elles l'aident à faire de l'excellente philosophie"), "Philosophie et christianisme: Note complémentaire," *Revue philosophique de Louvain*

he does not locate it in the formal or essential order but in that of mode or method. It is the way of philosophizing or "intellectual style" that was in vogue in patristic and medieval times and that created such brilliant philosophies as those of Augustine, Bonaventure or Aquinas. In order to appreciate this Christian way of doing philosophy one must abandon an essentialist way of thinking and approach it from an historical perspective. Christian philosophy then appears as "a complex historical reality, that of a revelation which is productive of human reasoning."[18]

For many years Gilson conceived Christian philosophy principally in terms of its relation to Christian faith. From the start he was aware that theology had a central role to play in forming Christian philosophical notions. "The deepest of them," he wrote in *The Spirit of Mediaeval Philosophy*, "have often to be disentangled from the theological contexts in which they are embedded, for it is there, in the bosom of theology, that they effectively come to birth."[19] He had a long way to go, however, before he arrived at a clear view of the nature of scholastic and Thomistic theology and the way it can give rise to rational philosophical doctrines. His odyssey can be traced through the successive editions of *Le thomisme*, from the first in 1919 to the sixth in 1965. In a letter dated 1959, when he was seventy-five years old, he wrote that he had spent a life "in rediscovering the true meaning of the word 'theology.'"[20] The fruits of that discovery are found in his books of the 1960s, including *Christian Philosophy*.

At first Gilson accepted the usual distinction between theology and philosophy based on their different methods of proof. In the discussion of Christian philosophy in 1933 he stated bluntly:

---

89 (1991): 499–505 at p. 504. Gilson, with Leo XIII, would say that revealed truths help the Christian philosopher to produce not just an excellent philosophy but the best.

18. Gilson's comments in *Bulletin de la Société française de philosophie* 31 (1931): 39; see also *The Philosopher and Theology*, pp. 192–193.

19. *Spirit of Mediaeval Philosophy*, p. 38; see also *Christianity and Philosophy*, pp. 82–102.

20. Gilson, in a letter dated 22 July 1959; quoted in Laurence K. Shook, *Etienne Gilson*, The Etienne Gilson Series 6 (Toronto: Pontifical Institute of Mediaeval Studies, 1984), p. 345.

"Theology does not demonstrate conclusions philosophically; philosophy does not deduce its conclusions from faith." Elaborating on this theme, he continues, "The conclusion of the theologian is always concerned with what is revealed, whatever appeal he might make to reason. The conclusion of the philosopher is always concerned with what is rationally demonstrated, whatever appeal he might make to faith." To which he adds that the theologian can sometimes become a bit of a philosopher and demonstrate a revealed truth, as St. Thomas did when he demonstrated the existence of God in his *Summa theologiae*.[21] But Gilson did not enlighten his audience as to how and why a rational demonstration of this sort could find a place in theology. In his *Reason and Revelation in the Middle Ages*, written a few years later (1938), he asserts that St. Thomas excluded from theology all necessary demonstrations of a purely rational nature. This is because the conclusions of theology follow from principles that are articles of faith.[22]

Twenty-five years later Gilson called this notion of theology "a very widespread illusion."[23] With a deeper understanding of scholastic theology, and especially Thomism, he saw that theological conclusions need not follow from premises, at least one of which comes from revelation. A conclusion demonstrated from two rational premises can be theological if it is used by the theologian as a means of understanding the faith. When a theologian uses rational demonstrations in this way, he is not being a bit of a philosopher (*un peu philosophe*), but a theologian in the full exercise of his science. Conclusions of philosophy, and indeed of all the sciences, can enter into theology, not as actually revealed (*revelata*), but at least as possible objects of revelation (*revelabilia*), for all truths can be revealed by God. Under the title of "reveal-

21. Gilson in the discussion following Aimé Forest's report "Le problème historique de la philosophie chrétienne," in *La philosophie chrétienne*, in *Journées d'études de la Société thomiste* 2 (1933): 71.

22. Gilson, *Reason and Revelation in the Middle Ages* (New York: Scribners, 1938), pp. 76, 78.

23. Gilson, *The Philosopher and Theology*, p. 97.

able," all natural truths fall within the scope of theology as means to achieve its end.[24]

Theology (or *sacra doctrina*), as Gilson understood it in his later years, is a transcendent science. Indeed, as St. Thomas says, it is an imprint in the human mind of God's own knowledge of things.[25] By analogy with the divine knowledge, theology "contains all human science by mode of eminence, to the extent at least to which it deems it advisable to incorporate it within itself and make it serve its own ends."[26] Philosophy is present in theology as its handmaid, preserving its own rationality there in order to be of service to theology. And yet, as incorporated into theology and used by it, it is part of theology. When St. Thomas was reproached for using pagan philosophical notions in his theology, thereby diluting the wine of scripture with the water of philosophy, he retorted: "Those who use the works of the philosophers in sacred doctrine, by bringing them into the service of faith, do not mix water with wine, but rather change water into wine."[27]

When philosophy is incorporated in theology, as it is in the theology of St. Thomas and other scholastic theologians, it can be viewed from two different angles. As philosophy, it retains its essential rationality, deepened and enlightened by the higher wisdom in which it dwells. Thus Gilson insists that the theology of St. Thomas "includes, not only in fact but necessarily, a strictly

24. Gilson, *The Philosopher and Theology*, pp. 97–98. For the notion of "the revealable" see Aquinas, *ST* 1.1.3 ad 2m, and Gilson's *Elements of Christian Philosophy*, pp. 34–35 and *The Christian Philosophy of St. Thomas Aquinas*, pp. 9–14.

25. *ST* 1.1.3 ad 2m; see below p. 42 and Gilson, *The Philosopher and Theology*, p. 100. On the nature of sacred doctrine (*sacra doctrina*) see Gilson's *Elements of Christian Philosophy*, pp. 22–42 and *The Christian Philosophy of St. Thomas Aquinas*, pp. 7–15.

26. Gilson, *The Philosopher and Theology*, p. 100.

27. Aquinas, *Expositio super librum Boethii de Trinitate*, 2.3 ad 5m, ed. Bruno Decker, Studien und Texte zur Geistesgeschichte des Mittelalters (Leiden: Brill, 1955), p. 96, trans. Armand Maurer as *Thomas Aquinas: Faith, Reason and Theology*, Mediaeval Sources in Translation 32 (Toronto: Pontifical Institute of Mediaeval Studies, 1987), p. 50. See also Gilson, *The Philosopher and Theology*, p. 101.

rational philosophy."[28] But that same philosophy is theological when it enters into the service of theology, for then it belongs to its household.[29] Formally distinct as philosophy and theology, these two different wisdoms intimately collaborate with each other without any confusion between them. With the help of philosophy, theology achieves the structure and status of a science, and it gains a deeper understanding of the contents of faith. Philosophy in turn benefits from its service to theology; for example, metaphysics makes deeper progress in understanding the primary notion of being.[30]

In line with the dual role of philosophy in theology, Gilson in his later writings describes Christian philosophy in two different but complementary ways. From the perspective of philosophy he defines it as "that way of philosophizing in which the Christian faith and the human intellect join forces in a common investigation of philosophical truth."[31] However, when philosophy is viewed as a handmaid of theology, and consequently as having the same end as theology, it is defined as "the investigation, by means of philosophy, of the saving truth revealed by God and accessible to the light of natural reason."[32] Christian philosophy, then, in its own modest way brings with it an invaluable understanding of the word of God.

In Gilson's view, the close association of Christian or scholastic metaphysics with theology is not simply a fact observable in medieval thought; it belongs to the very essence of that metaphysics. Medieval philosophy, he insists, owed its fecundity to the service it gave to theologians. As theologians used philosophy in the light of faith they transformed philosophy. They did not begin with contemporary philosophies and adapt theology to them; neither Duns Scotus nor Thomas Aquinas based their theologies on any philosophy, not even that of Aristotle. They started with

28. Gilson, *Le thomisme,* p. 7.
29. See below p. 28, and Gilson, *The Philosopher and Theology,* p. 101.
30. See below pp. 31–32. With one and the same movement the mind achieves a deeper insight into the notion of being and gains a better knowledge of the faith.
31. Gilson, *Elements of Christian Philosophy,* p. 5.
32. Gilson, "What Is Christian Philosophy?" p. 187.

faith, and while appropriating current philosophical notions, they developed them in the light of faith. If scholastic philosophy in the future is to be original and creative, it must be true to its essence and remain closely allied with theology.[33]

Some historians agree with Gilson that the great medieval schoolmen were influenced by their Christian faith, but they deny his further claim that their philosophies owe their excellence to their presence within theology. As these scholars see it, Aquinas developed his original philosophy, and especially his metaphysics, before he began his work as a theologian and as a necessary condition for it. So we should not say, with Gilson, that Aquinas was a great philosopher because he was a great theologian; the opposite is nearer the truth.[34] In fact, however, the chronology of Aquinas's writings does not support the view that his philosophical development preceded his theological endeavors. His earliest major production – the *Commentary on the Sentences* (1252–1256) – is not a philosophical but a theological work. His first philosophical treatises, like *De principiis naturae* and *De ente et essentia*, do not antedate the commentary but are contemporary with it.[35] It appears, then, that Aquinas elaborated his philosophy along with his theology, while using it as its instrument.

Gilson finds in history the lesson that metaphysics needs theology. The theologians of the Middle Ages produced a variety of metaphysics as their instruments. With Descartes the ties between religion and metaphysics were cut, as metaphysics prided itself with dispensing with the theology from which it came. Metaphysics then lost its sense of identity, and philosophy took

33. See Etienne Gilson, "Historical Research and the Future of Scholasticism," *The Modern Schoolman* 29 (1951): 1–10, reprinted in *A Gilson Reader*, ed. Pegis, pp. 156–167.

34. See Fernand Van Steenberghen, *La philosophie au XIII*e* siècle*, Philosophes médiévaux 9 (Louvain: Publications Universitaires, 1966), pp. 350–354; and Wippel, *Metaphysical Themes in Thomas Aquinas*, p. 29 with n80.

35. I am following the chronology of Thomas's works in James A. Weisheipl, *Friar Thomas d'Aquino: His Life, Thought, and Work* (Garden City, New York: Doubleday, 1974; with corrigenda and addenda, Washington, DC: The Catholic University of America Press, 1983).

up arms against it with Kant's critique and Comte's positivism. Metaphysics died at their hands, and the condition of its revival is the return to theology.[36]

Gilson knew that his appeal to scholastic philosophers to return to theology would not be popular. They would be offended to hear that their philosophy should be in some way directed and enlightened by theology. Would this not mean the loss of philosophy's freedom and independence? And yet, Gilson insisted, theology helped to produce outstanding philosophies in the Middle Ages and it can do so again in the twentieth century. The restoration he called for will not mean the loss of metaphysics; rather, scholastic philosophers will lose their metaphysics by losing their theology.[37]

It is true that in the Middle Ages Christian philosophy was the work of theologians, created as an instrument of their theology. In that condition, as Gilson's colleague Anton Pegis pointed out, Christian philosophy "was a religious tool and, by so much, not a philosophy but a theology." It "did not, in fact, have the autonomous state of expression proper to a philosophy."[38] Is Christian philosophy possible today as the work, not of theologians but philosophers, yet closely engaged with Christian faith and theology? Pegis thought so, and as far as I know Gilson never disagreed with him in this matter. Since Christian philosophy is not *a* philosophy but a *way* of philosophizing, Gilson thought it could take many forms. He praised Jacques Maritain and Gabriel Marcel, whose Christian existentialisms were not developed as handmaids of theology but nevertheless had close ties with faith and, at least in Maritain's case, with theology.[39] Gilson himself, when writing as a philosopher, practiced the same style of Christian philosophy, using methods proper to philosophy but never far

36. See below pp. 128, 133–134.

37. See below pp. 133–134, and Gilson, "Historical Research and the Future of Scholasticism."

38. Anton C. Pegis, *The Middle Ages and Philosophy* (Chicago: Henry Regnery, 1963), pp. 71–72.

39. See *Jacques Maritain, son oeuvre philosophique*, présentation d'Etienne Gilson (Paris: Desclée de Brouwer, 1948), and *Existentialisme chrétienne: Gabriel Marcel*, présentation d'Etienne Gilson, textes de Jeanne Delhomme et al. (Paris: Plon, 1948).

from scripture and theology.[40] But Gilson himself does not claim to know what forms Christian philosophy will assume in the years to come: that remains "a secret of the future."[41]

The fact remains that Gilson's ideal form of Christian philosophy, as most productive of original philosophical and especially metaphysical ideas, was that of medieval theologians like Thomas Aquinas. They brought philosophy into theology as its servant, but Gilson did not regard its service in theology as demeaning or harmful to it. On the contrary philosophy gained a greater dignity and status in the household of theology: it was able to see further and to demonstrate truths inaccessible to it before.

The pivotal notion in *Christian Philosophy* is 'being,' understood in the Thomistic sense as 'the act of existing' (*actus essendi*). It is implied by all the other concepts elucidated in the book, like 'cause,' 'substance,' and 'essence.' Aquinas has been criticized for speaking of being as an act, but this is justified by the fact that 'being' (*ens*) is a participle derived from the verb 'to be' (*esse*). It is like the participle 'running' (*currens*), derived from the verb 'to run' (*currere*). As 'running' denotes the act of running, so by analogy 'being' denotes the act of being or existing. Aquinas also uses both *ens* and *esse* as verbal nouns. Then *ens* signifies concretely 'that which is' while *esse* signifies the act of being in abstraction from the subject exercising the act. Similarly *currens* can be used as a noun, signifying 'one who runs' or 'a runner,' while *currere* can signify the act of running without the person who runs.[42] Translating this into English, we can say that 'a

40. Gilson's books on language and evolution are examples of the living Thomism he advocated: *Linguistique et philosophie: Essai sur les constantes philosophiques du langage* (Paris: Vrin, 1969); *D'Aristote à Darwin et retour: Essai sur quelques constantes de la biophilosophie* (Paris: Vrin, 1971), trans. John Lyon as *From Aristotle to Darwin and Back Again: A Journey in Final Causality, Species and Evolution* (Notre Dame, Ind.: University of Notre Dame Press, 1984). See *The Spirit of Thomism*, The Fenwick Lectures in Philosophy (New York: Kenedy & Sons, 1964), pp. 84–102.

41. See Gilson, *The Philosopher and Theology*, p. 217.

42. See Aquinas, *Expositio libri Boetii De Ebdomadibus* 2, ed. Louis J. Bataillon and Carlo A. Grassi in the Leonine *Opera omnia*, vol. 50 (Rome: Commissio Leonina; Paris: Editions du Cerf, 1992), p. 271.48–59.

being' (*ens*) is 'that which exists,' and 'being' or 'existing' (*esse*) is the act whereby it exists.

In the metaphysics of Aquinas every finite being is composed of an act of existing and an essence that limits the act and gives the being its specific nature. Thus in its metaphysical structure a human being contains an act of existing rendered human by the essence 'humanity.' The whole reality of the being, including its essence, is owing to the act whereby it exists, for unless it exists it is nothing. Hence the act of existing, rather than essence or substance, is at the very core of a being; in Aquinas's words, it is "the actuality of all acts and consequently the perfection of all perfections" (*QDP* 7.2 ad 9).

Can the metaphysician demonstrate this? In particular, can he demonstrate the real composition of being and essence in finite beings? In Chapter 6 Gilson reviews the proofs that are usually given, but he finds none truly demonstrative. He sees them as either dialectical or presupposing the notion of being as the act of existing (*esse*). The most convincing begins with the proposition that God is the pure act of existing (*ipsum purum esse*). Since creatures are not God, they cannot *be* the act of existing but must *have* it in finite measure, determined by their essences. Hence they must be really composed of *esse* and essence.

Gilson finds the argument "rational and properly philosophical in structure," but he points out that the revelation of the divine name as 'He Who Is,' "directs it, guides it, and leads it finally to its goal."[43] In short, Gilson regards the argument as a prime example of Christian philosophy. Because God revealed his proper name as 'He Who Is' or 'I Am,' the Christian metaphysician is led to conceive God as pure Being. In Augustine's striking interpretation, he is 'Is' (*est est*).[44] But whereas Augustine understood this to mean that God is the supreme immutable essence, Aquinas renders the divine name as the pure act of existing. From this it is but a short step to conceive God's primal gift to creatures as a sharing in the divine act of existing in a measure determined by their finite essences.

43. Below, p. 28.
44. See below p. 73 with n18. For Augustine's understanding of God as pure being, see also below p. 53.

Gilson was well aware that today many do not accept Aquinas's reading of the divine name in Exodus 3:14–15. Philologists point out that God's revelation to Moses, rendered 'I Am Who Am,' derives from the Greek Septuagint translation of the Bible. The Hebrew reads: 'I Am Who I Am,' or 'I Am What I Am,' suggesting that God intended to conceal rather than reveal his name to Moses. Gilson does not dispute the competence of philologists to settle the matter, though he points out that not all agree on the reading of the Hebrew. God may have wanted to veil the mystery of his divinity, Gilson continues, but he also intended to reply to Moses's request for his name. So God immediately gave Moses the names 'I Am' and 'Yahweh (He Is).' It will be recalled that this is the divine name Jesus gave himself when he said to the Jews: "... before Abraham was, I am" (John 8:58).[45]

Gilson grants that these passages of scripture are intended to convey a religious and not a philosophical message. And yet he does not agree with scripture scholars who deny that the metaphysical speculations of the church fathers and medieval schoolmen regarding the divine name of Being are without foundation in the sacred text. Like any work of literature, the text of Exodus is open to many literal interpretations. In the present case, the text is divinely inspired, and it can contain meanings beyond the reach of the philologists' methods of exegesis. In Gilson's view, the centuries-old theological speculation about Being as the proper name of God has not been futile or misguided. Sanctioned by the church, which through its tradition guarantees the correct interpretation of scripture, it has led to a deeper understanding of the revealed text and at the same time to a new existential notion of being.

Does the theologian really need the term 'being' in his discussion of God? Heidegger did not think so, and Jean-Luc Marion is sympathetic to this position in his recent book *God*

45. For Gilson's attitude toward philologists, see below pp. 25–26. Perhaps it is not out of place to add, in this connection, that, although scholastic theology flourished in the Middle Ages, biblical theology did not match strides with it. Bonaventure and Aquinas did not know the original languages of the Bible or contemporary literary forms, all of which are necessary for understanding the "sacred page."

without Being.[46] Marion concedes that Exodus 3:14 can be taken as a positive statement, "I am the One who is," but in the first place it should be read as "I am who I am" , that is, as a refusal on God's part to say who he is. Marion quotes with approval Gilson's statement that the sacred text "offers the only formula that says absolutely nothing (of God) and that says absolutely everything."[47] What is certain is that it says nothing definite about him. But when he is conceived as Being, Marion urges, the concept names and defines him, holds him within its grasp, freezes the divine in a concept, and implies the equivalence of God to a general concept. Thus 'being' functions as an idol; it is in fact an idolatrous concept: "When the idol appears, the gaze has just stopped: the idol concretizes that stop."[48]

To make matters worse, Marion sees Aquinas as introducing the imagination into the apprehension of being, thus submitting the concept "to the essence and to the marvels of representation." "This claim," he warns, "does not easily escape the suspicion of idolatry, as soon as the *ens*, thus referred to God, is engendered not only *in conceptione intellectus* but also *in imaginatione intellectus* – in the imagination of the understanding, hence in the faculty of forming images, hence idols."[49]

Some decades before Marion wrote his book Gilson effectively countered these views in *Christian Philosophy*. He makes it clear that to speak of God as Being is not to define him, for the notion of being is too simple and indeterminate to function as a definition.[50] As

46. Jean-Luc Marion, *God without Being: Hors-Texte*, trans. Thomas A. Carlson (Chicago: University of Chicago Press, 1991), esp. p. 61, where Marion cites a passage from Heidegger: "If I were yet to write a theology – to which I sometimes feel inclined – then the word *Being* would not occur in it. Faith does not need the thought of Being. When faith has recourse to this thought, it is no longer faith" (*Séminaire de Zurich*, French trans. by D. Saatdjian and F. Fédier, in *Poésie* 13 [1980]: 60–61).

47. Marion, *God without Being*, p. 79, citing Gilson's *L'Athéisme difficile* (Paris: Vrin, 1979), p. 59.

48. Marion, *God without Being*, p. 11.

49. Ibid., pp. 81–82.

50. See below p. 73. See also Etienne Gilson, "Yahweh et les grammairiens," in his *Constantes philosophiques de l'être*, avant-propos de

Thomas Aquinas shows, its very simplicity and generality are reasons for its suitability as the proper name of God: unlike other names it imposes on him no mode or measure of being (*ST* 1.13.11).

In his discussion of God does the metaphysician set up the concept of being as a kind of idol, where the mind stops? If this were the case, the metaphysician would not be a Thomist. Gilson points out that, in the doctrine of Thomas Aquinas, the object of metaphysics is not the concept of being as being, but existing being; otherwise metaphysics would be turned into logic and become an empty verbalism.[51] As Gilson says elsewhere, "... the concept cannot be the ultimate object of philosophy."[52] Through his conception of being the metaphysician grasps beings in their acts of existing and pursues the supreme existent, who is God.[53] We can know the divine being and other perfections only on the analogy of those of creatures, with the consequence "that none of the names we give to God, even if they are absolutely and positively true on the level of human knowledge, *represents* any perfection of God *such as it is in him*." Gilson expresses this limitation by the telling phrase "agnosticism of representation."[54]

Whether the most suitable name of God is 'He Who Is' or 'the Good,' as Marion prefers (following the Christian Neoplatonic tradition), the mystery of God remains intact. In the words of Thomas Aquinas, "We reach the peak of our knowledge of God when we know that we do not know him, in the sense that we know that what God is surpasses everything we know of him" (*QDP* 7.6 ad 14). Then, as Marion says, the proper attitude toward God is silence: not a silence in metaphysics but beyond it, when love is received as a gift of God and returned.[55] Although Gilson's position on God and being is the antithesis of Marion's, in the end they agree on the primacy of the love of God in the present life.

Jean-François Courtine, Bibliothèque des textes philosophiques (Paris: Vrin, 1983), pp. 231–253 at 233–234; and Gilson, *The Christian Philosophy of Saint Thomas Aquinas*, p. 91.

51. See below pp. 67–68.

52. Gilson, *The Christian Philosophy of Saint Thomas Aquinas*, p. 366.

53. Ibid., p. 44.

54. Below, p. 36; see also pp. 39–43.

55. Marion, *God without Being*, p. 107.

In the words of Gilson, "... in the last analysis, in this life we can only embrace God by love, beyond affirmations and negations, in darkness."[56]

A word concerning the translation of the language of being. Gilson renders *ens* by the neologism *étant*, and *esse* by *être*. I have translated *étant* by "a being" and *être* by "being."

Gilson appears to have written his *Christian Philosophy* while convalescing from an operation in January 1959.[57] During this period he wrote two other books. Perhaps this flurry of activity accounts for the lack of careful checking of references in *Christian Philosophy*. I have tried to correct faulty citations. I have translated Latin texts in footnotes or in parentheses after the texts. My own notes are placed in square brackets.

I am grateful to my Basilian confrères and professors of the Pontifical Institute of Mediaeval Studies for assistance in translating the book. A special word of thanks is due to Kevin J. Kirley, CSB, for checking the translation and making corrections and helpful suggestions. Of course the responsibility for the translation is mine.

ARMAND MAURER
Pontifical Institute of Mediaeval Studies
Toronto

October 1993

56. Below, p. 86; see p. 39. For the primacy of the love of God in this life see *ST* 1.82.3.

57. See Shook, *Etienne Gilson*, pp. 342–343.

Christian Philosophy

To the holy memory of
ABBÉ LUCIEN PAULET
born 7 October 1876
ordained priest 29 June 1901
professor at the Petit Séminaire de Paris
(1901–1905)
director at the Grand Séminaire de Paris
(1905–1907)
Aumônier militaire
awarded the Croix de Guerre
buried at the Champ d'Honneur
29 September 1915

Editions and Translations Consulted

For scriptural quotations, I have relied on the Revised Standard Version and the Douay–Rheims translation, sometimes adapting them to Gilson's own translations.

CCL   Corpus Christianorum: Series latina (Turnhout: Brepols, 1953–)

CG   Thomas Aquinas, *Summa contra Gentiles*, Leonine Manual Edition (Rome: Commissio Leonina, 1934) [trans. Anton C. Pegis et al. as *On the Truth of the Catholic Faith*, 5 vols. (Garden City, New York: Doubleday, 1955–1957)]

DM   Francisco Suárez, *Disputationes metaphysicae*, ed. Carlo Barton, vols. 25, 26 (1861, 1877) in *Opera omnia*, ed. D.M. André, 26 vols. (Paris: Vivès, 1856–1894)

EE   Thomas Aquinas, *De ente et essentia*, in *Le 'De ente et essentia' de s. Thomas d'Aquin: Texte établi d'après les manuscrits parisiens: Introduction, notes et études historiques* by M.-D. Roland-Gosselin, Bibliothèque thomiste 8 (1926; Paris: Vrin, 1948) [trans. Armand A. Maurer as *On Being and Essence*, 2nd ed., Mediaeval Sources in Translation 1 (Toronto: Pontifical Institute of Mediaeval Studies, 1968)]

PL   Patrologiae cursus completus: Series latina, ed. J.-P. Migne, 221 vols. (Paris: Migne, 1844–1891)

QDP   Thomas Aquinas, *Quaestiones disputatae: De potentia*, ed. Paul M. Pession, 9th ed. (Turin: Marietti, 1953) [trans. English Dominican Fathers (Laurence Shapcote) as *On the Power of God*, 3 vols. (London: 1932–1934), repr. in 1 vol. (Westminster, Maryland: The Newman Press, 1952)]

QDV   Thomas Aquinas, *Quaestiones disputatae: De veritate*, ed. Antoine Dondaine in the Leonine *Opera omnia*, vol. 22.1–3 (Rome: Editori di San Tommaso, 1970–1976) [trans. Robert M. Mulligan, James V. McGlynn, and Robert W. Schmidt as *Truth*, 3 vols. (Chicago: Henry Regnery, 1952–1954)]

ST   Thomas Aquinas, *Summa theologiae*, ed. Institutum Studiorum Medievalium Ottaviensis, 5 vols. (Ottawa: Studium Generalis O. Pr., 1941–1945) [Latin text and English translation, introduction, notes, appendices, and glossaries, by Thomas Gilby et al., 61 vols. (Cambridge: Blackfriars; New York: McGraw-Hill, 1964–1981)]

Preface

By "Christian philosophy" we shall mean the way of philosophizing described under this name by Pope Leo XIII in the encyclical *Aeterni Patris*. As its model he gave the doctrine of St. Thomas Aquinas.[1]

St. Thomas has been highly praised, and never more than he deserves, but not always correctly understood. The criticisms levelled against him have been sharp and sometimes very harsh. Those prompted by a sincere love of the truth have done no harm. Even when they lacked a solid basis, they have set their readers, sometimes even their authors, on the road to truth. The most damaging are those which, given out as accepted truths by constant repetition, obscure the meaning of the doctrine, distort its nature, and turn away from its study so many minds it could nourish, so many souls it might help along the road to salvation.

Among these criticisms there is one we would hardly dare to mention, since it concerns a saint and doctor whom the Church has chosen as the patron of its schools, and whose doctrine it has recommended as the rule and norm of its own teaching in theol-

---

1. [The term "Christian philosophy" does not appear in the encyclical, but a year later in an apostolic letter the Pope gave his encyclical the title "De philosophia christiana ad mentem s. Thomae Aquinatis Doctoris Angelici in scholis catholicis instauranda" (On the restoration of Christian philosophy in Catholic schools according to the mind of St. Thomas Aquinas, the Angelic Doctor): *Acta sanctae sedis* 13 (1880): 56–59 at p. 56. See *The Church Speaks to the Modern World: The Social Teachings of Leo XIII*, edited, annotated and with an introduction by Etienne Gilson (Garden City, New York: Image Books, Doubleday, 1954), p. 39. For the authenticity of the title see Georges Van Riet, "Le titre de l'encyclique 'Aeterni Patris': Note historique," *Revue philosophique de Louvain* 80 (1982): 35–63.]

ogy and philosophy.[2] Nevertheless we hear it said of scholastic
theology in general that it was harmful to Christian truth because
it substitutes reason for faith, philosophy for revelation, pride of
knowing for love and saving piety. St. Thomas has taken his
share of these criticisms in proportion to his authority in theology,
which is not slight. But there has never been an objection more
completely wide of the mark. It would take a long time to ferret
out the origins of this mistake, and in any case the conclusions
would remain uncertain. The purpose of our little book is simply
to show the contrary: that the theology of St. Thomas Aquinas,
far from excluding spirituality, is in fact a spirituality.

This ought to be self-evident. The theology of a theologian
worthy of the name cannot be anything but the very movement
of his mind and love as he seeks the truth about God in the
teaching of sacred scripture and in the study of his creatures.
Such is the theology of St. Thomas Aquinas. True, its technical
rigor and the high degree of abstraction of its basic notions make
it difficult for everyone to enter into it, and practically impossible
for some, but this difficulty does not change its object or its
purpose. There is no warrant in thinking that this purpose, which
is an understanding of faith (*intellectus fidei*), is beyond the reach
of minds capable of grasping its terms. Even when they were
repelled by the dryness and the intricacy of its technical proofs,
the light of truth that spontaneously bursts upon minds should
have been to some extent perceptible to them in the propositions
in which it is expressed.

Some of these propositions are set forth here for meditation.
Their choice is entirely my own. Above all I want to highlight
certain basic notions that dominate St. Thomas's teaching and
assure its intelligibility. For reasons that will be given, St. Thomas
did not want to compress his theology into a system that would

2. [Papal statements to this effect are conveniently collected in
Jacques Maritain, *St. Thomas Aquinas,* trans. Joseph W. Evans and Peter
O'Reilly (New York: Meridian Books, 1958). Vatican II gives testimony
to the value of St. Thomas's thought. See "Decree on Priestly Formation" §16 and "Declaration on Christian Education" §10 in *The Documents of Vatican II,* gen. ed. Walter M. Abbott (New York: Herder &
Herder, Association Press, 1966), pp. 452, 648.]

include only the most personal features of his philosophical thought. As a result, what is most original in his teaching is so to speak drowned in a sea of doctrines which it cannot be said are not his own, but which are his only because he first made them so. My purpose here is to set forth clearly the notions that are basic and in a sense Thomist by birth, and that alone enable us to understand the use St. Thomas makes of the others. They can be recognized by the fact that without them there would be no Thomism as a distinct and personal doctrine of St. Thomas Aquinas. The other notions entering into the texture of his work and enhancing its richness are Thomistic only because of them.

Besides these general reasons, the choice we have made of master themes expresses a spontaneous preference for certain statements and features of the thought of the Common Doctor of the Church.

The writer who reports them has never been able to reread them without having the impression of their leading him as close to God as is possible for a human mind to approach him while meditating on the meaning of his word. My only desire is to share that experience with others. It will never be a question of demonstrating, but only of showing, leaving to each reader the task of finding his own way and trying in his own fashion to approach the sublime mysteries whose neglect would be the death of metaphysics as well as of theology, and whose meditation, in the humility of love, is a work of piety no less than of wisdom. Among so many ways to God, no one of which is useless, it is good that this one also remains an option: not a way of science or scholarship or even of reading, but rather a series of meditations, freely made by each reader in his own fashion on theological themes borrowed from St. Thomas and proposed for the mind's reflection.

1

Philosophizing within Faith

Sed contra est quod dicitur Exod. 3 ex persona Dei: *Ego sum qui sum (Summa theologiae* 1.2.3)[1]

Theologians often quote this statement of God to establish, on the basis of belief in divine authority, that Being is the proper name of God. Here, however, it is found in the second question of the *Summa theologiae,* in the *sed contra* of article 3: "Is there a God?"; or, as we usually say, "Does God exist?"

Since it is taken from scripture, the statement certainly means that God himself has given an affirmative answer to the question of his existence. To assent to his word is to believe that God exists because he himself has said so. In this sense the existence of God is held as true through an act of faith in the word of God.

The knowledge of God's existence thereby acquires a universal significance and absolute certitude. Indeed, even those who do not understand the philosophical proofs of the existence of God are informed about this truth by divine revelation. Philosophers or not, everyone to whom his word is communicated through the preaching of scripture and who receives it as coming from him, in this way knows that God exists. Philosophers themselves need to remember that God has revealed his existence and to hold onto that truth by faith.

There are rational proofs by which we can know with certitude that God exists; but the certitude of faith, which is based on the infallibility of the word of God,[2] is infinitely more reliable

1. ["On the contrary, the book of Exodus (3:14) presents God as saying *I am who am.*"]

2. "... much more is a person certain about what he hears from God, who cannot be mistaken, than about what he sees with his own reason, which can be mistaken" (*ST* 2–2.4.8 ad 2m). [Gilson then adds the following quotation:] "In reply to the third objection we say that

than all knowledge acquired by natural reason alone, no matter how evident it may be. In matters of revelation, error is absolutely impossible because the source of the knowledge of faith is God himself, who is the Truth.

Important consequences follow from this, the first of which is that the theologian, as he begins his work, by calling upon the word of God affirming his own existence, asserts in the name of faith the existence of the proper object of theological science. In this sense the whole of theology hangs upon that first truth – a point worthy of meditation.

There were prophets who in certain respects could have been greater than Moses, but absolutely speaking Moses remains the greatest of all: *Non surrexit propheta ultra in Israel, sicut Moyses* (And there has not arisen a prophet since in Israel like Moses; Deut. 34:10). Scripture immediately gives the reason for this judgment. There has not arisen in Israel a prophet equal to Moses, "he whom Yahweh knew face to face." St. Thomas will look no further for the first reason for his own position that Moses excelled all the prophets (*ST* 2–2.174.4). There are four special signs of prophecy: knowledge both by intellectual and imaginative insight, the promulgation of revealed truth, and the confirmation of that promulgation by miracles. The first two of these four signs should hold our attention here. First, Moses excels the other

---

understanding and science are more perfect than the knowledge of faith because they have a greater clarity, but not because they have a greater certitude. For the whole certitude of understanding or science, as gifts [of the Holy Spirit], comes from the certitude of faith, as the certitude of the knowledge of conclusions comes from the certitude of principles. But insofar as science, wisdom, and understanding are [natural] intellectual virtues, they are based on the natural light of reason, which falls short of the certitude of God's word, on which faith is based" (*ST* 2–2.4.8 ad 3m). So it seems impossible to acquire in the light of principles of knowledge themselves certitudes equal to those given by faith in the word of God, for this word expresses the certitude that God himself has. Now this certitude is infallible, whereas that of the finite natural light is not. Hence in no case would reason be substituted for faith without changing the less infallibly certain for the more infallibly certain.

prophets by his intellectual vision of God, since, like St. Paul later in his rapture, "he saw the essence itself of God." But he also had the sensible perception of it to a degree attained by no other prophet, for he enjoyed it so to speak at will, not only hearing God's words but even seeing God himself speak, either in sleep or even while awake. In the face-to-face vision of the divine essence Moses saw that God exists. Hence it is by an act of faith in that existence of God revealed to Moses in an immediate vision that the theologian first answers the question, Does God exist? Nothing will ever replace for us the assent to that intellectual vision of the divine essence that Moses had face to face and in which we ourselves can share, obscurely but infallibly, by faith.

St. Thomas never doubted the necessity of believing in the existence of the God of Moses at the beginning of all theological inquiry. According to him, faith consists principally in two things: the true knowledge of God and the mystery of the Incarnation. Now, there can be no hesitation about what he calls the true knowledge of God. By that he understands what *all* the faithful are bound to believe *explicitly* and *always* in order to be saved. These are the truths spoken of by the Apostle in the *Epistle to the Hebrews*, 11.6: "Without faith it is impossible to please him. For whoever would draw near to God must believe that he exists and that he rewards those who seek him." To which St. Thomas adds, "Consequently everyone (*quilibet*) is bound to believe *explicitly* and *always* that God exists (*Deum esse*) and that he exercises his providence over human affairs" (*QDV* 14.11). So all our theological knowledge of God begins with an act of faith in God's revelation of his own existence. The *Ego sum* of Exodus is indeed in its right place in the *Summa theologiae*, before all the rational and properly philosophical proofs of the existence of God.

At this point we should carefully avoid a confusion that is all too prevalent. How, it will be asked, could the theologian at one and the same time believe that God exists and rationally demonstrate his existence? The question seems to be all the more in order as St. Thomas himself explicitly teaches that it is impossible to believe and to know the same conclusion at the same time and in the same respect. Will it be necessary, then, to stop believing that God exists after having demonstrated his existence five times; or, on the contrary, will we pretend to continue believing what we already knew? If we remove belief in the existence of God, we assign to theology an object whose very existence is established by philosophy, but if we keep it after the demonstration we are asked to believe what we know, which is impossible.

In order to clear up this difficulty, we must remember first of all what the object of faith is, namely the substance or foundation of the whole spiritual edifice. Faith is not directed to the formula of the proposition that calls for our assent. Beyond the intelligible meaning of the words it directly reaches the very object which these words signify. For this reason alone no rational proof of the truth of the proposition "God exists" could dispense us from believing in the existence of him in whom we believe on the word of God. Affirming God by faith is specifically different from affirming him by philosophical reason. The truth of the conclusion of the philosopher is justified on its own rational ground; the affirmation of the faithful is a sharing in the knowledge that God himself has of his own existence and of which he instructs us by way of revelation. Faith is a properly *theological* virtue which has God for its cause and object.

Accordingly, the knowledge of faith and the knowledge of reason do not belong to the same species, not even to the same genus. Knowledge of the existence of God as an assent to the revelation made to us about it is entirely different from that which philosophy conveys about it, because for the believer it is a first real possession of God and his first step on the road to his final end – the beatific vision. Between the face-to-face vision of Moses and that of eternal life, faith offers to believers an obscure but certain road that does not lead to metaphysics but to salvation. Hence God only revealed his existence to us because he began, in that free initiative, to give us already in an obscure way a sort of laying hold of our final end: *accedentem ad Deum oportet credere quia est* (whoever would draw near to God must believe that he exists: Heb 11:6). No philosophy, no natural knowledge of God, could put us in possession, whether it be by one or five ways, of a knowledge of God's existence that belongs to the economy of salvation. Philosophy is not a doctrine of salvation. We should not lose sight of this absolute transcendence of theological knowledge and of faith: "The principal object of faith is the First Truth, the vision of which gives the happiness of heaven and takes the place of faith" (*Principale objectum fidei est veritas prima, cujus visio beatos facit et fidei succedit*: ST 2–2.5.1). Hence the relation of belief in

God's existence to the certain knowledge of it given by philosophical demonstrations does not truly raise any insoluble problem.

Some are upset to hear that natural reason is fallible, even when it makes use of first principles. It is simply a fact that it makes mistakes. It is certain that the existence of God is rationally demonstrable, but not all the demonstrations of it that are offered are conclusive. Suppose a philosopher like St. Anselm holds it for certain that God exists on the ground of the purely rational conclusion that we cannot know the meaning of the word "God" without being compelled to admit his existence, not only in thought but also in reality.[3] The least we can say is that the proof is not certainly conclusive. If it were not, what would be the position of a philosopher, in this case one who is also a theologian and a saint, who would think himself dispensed from believing that God exists, with the excuse that he knows it with certainty by a rational demonstration whose value in fact is uncertain? He would no longer believe in the existence of God, but he would believe he knows it, and since he would neither believe it nor know it, that person would be completely ignorant of the existence of God. That truth is then no longer recognized except in the confused way described by St. Thomas (*ST* 1.2.1 ad 1m), or by a belief that takes itself for knowledge: *partim ex consuetudine* (*CG* 1.11.1). Certitude, which is our concern here, does not belong to judgments of this sort, and that is why the only infallible and supremely reliable certitude remains that of the act of faith. It is always present and is never mistaken.

So we must try to distinguish between two questions that are often confused in this discussion. Is the existence of God a truth demonstrable by natural reason, so that it is knowable and known with certitude? Without a doubt the answer to this first question is "yes." The second question is whether everyone can consider his natural reason infallible in its effort to demonstrate rationally the existence of God? The merciless criticism of the proofs of St. Augustine, St. Anselm, Descartes, Malebranche and many others

3. [Anselm, *Proslogium* 2, in *Opera omnia*, ed. Francis S. Schmitt, 6 vols. (Seckau: Abbatial; Edinburgh: Thomas Nelson, 1938–1961), 1: 101–102.]

are timely reminders of the need for modesty. Are we keener philosophers than they? That is the whole question. Modesty is not skepticism. So we should not be afraid to let our mind pursue the proof of God's existence until we reach the greatest possible certitude, but we should keep intact our faith in the word that reveals this truth to the most simple folk as well as to the most learned.[4]

Others are also concerned that if we adopt this attitude, we are once again involved in the contradiction already mentioned, that is, knowing and believing one and the same proposition. But this is not the case. By a supernatural act of faith we cannot believe that God is the immovable Prime Mover, or the First Efficient Cause, or the First Necessary Being. All this, which the philosopher demonstrates, belongs to natural reason, not to faith. These conclusions, moreover, have been discovered by men like Aristotle and Avicenna; they have not been revealed by God. It is true that if the God of revelation exists, he is the Prime Mover, the First Efficient Cause, the First Necessary Being, and everything reason can prove about the First Cause of the universe. But if Yahweh is the Prime Mover, the Prime Mover is not Yahweh. The First Efficient Cause never spoke to me by his prophets, and I do not expect my salvation to come from him. The God in whose existence the faithful believe infinitely transcends the one whose existence is proved by the philosopher. Above all, he is a God of whom philosophy could have no idea, for all the conclusions of natural theology only reveal to us the existence of a First Cause of the universe. They are affirmed as the crowning point of science, but along the same line, whereas Yahweh reveals his existence to us in order to raise us to the vision of his essence and to share his own happiness with us. The God of reason is the God of science; the God of faith is the God of salvation. All the philosophical demonstrations can easily unfold below that divine reve-

4. Here it is well to meditate on the very complex and nuanced passage in *ST* 2–2.2.4: "Is it necessary to believe what can be proved by natural reason?" The answer is in the affirmative: "We must accept by faith not only what is above reason but also what can be known by reason."

lation; no one of them could reach it or even conceive of its object.

So we believe all the knowledge that directs us to beatitude, and all knowledge is the object of faith insofar as it directs us to beatitude. All *scibilia* are alike in being objects of knowledge, but because all do not equally direct us to beatitude not all are equally *credenda* (*ST* 2–2.2.4 ad 3m). Knowing the existence of God because it can be proved in the Aristotelian manner does not even start us on the road to salvation; believing that God exists because he has revealed it sets us on the road to our final end. Then there is nothing to prevent the theologian from directing all his knowledge toward that end, including Aristotle, Avicenna, Averroes, and the storehouse of their proofs. Philosophy can and ought to be saved, but it could not save itself any more than the philosopher could. As philosophy, it cannot even conceive the simple possibility of its own salvation.

We can recognize the absolute transcendence of revelation by the curious fact of the philosophical and theological multiple meanings of the texts of scripture. When St. Thomas was looking for a *sed contra* for his question on the existence of God, he does not seem to have found a text in which Yahweh says in so many words, "I exist." So he had recourse to the statement of Exodus: *Ego sum qui sum*. But that statement is a reply to the question Moses put to God: When the people ask me who has sent me to them, what shall I answer? So the passage in question also contains the reply to another query: What is the proper name of God? This question will be raised later in the *Summa* 1.13.11, and the *sed contra* will simply appeal to another part of the same text (Exod. 3:14): "Say this to the children of Israel: 'I Am' has sent me to you." The text of the *Summa* reads: "... respondit ei Dominus: *Sic dices eis: Qui est misit me ad vos*. Ergo hoc nomen *Qui est* est maxime proprium nomen Dei" (The Lord answered him, 'This is what you shall say to them: He Who Is sent me to you.' Therefore this name, He Who Is, is the most proper name of God). Hence the *sed contra* that guarantees the existence of God has a wealth of meaning of which none of the five ways of proving that existence could give the slightest idea. The God of the *sed contra* is someone, a person, who reveals his name while revealing his existence. These matters do not come within the scope of philosophy. It is not called upon here to prove the truth of scripture. The theologian asks for its help only to put humankind on the track of an order of whose existence it itself has no suspicion and consequently to which it will never have access.[5]

A written statement almost incidentally casts a still more instructive light on what the mind of the theologian can read in a single word if it is spoken by God. In the article of the *Summa* in which St. Thomas asks if the degrees of prophecy vary with the passage of time, he answers in the affirmative, and he offers the following proof: "The Fathers who had gone before had been instructed in the faith about the omnipotence of the one God, but afterward Moses was more fully taught about the simplicity of the divine essence when he was told *Ego sum qui sum*, the name the Jews represented by the term 'Adonai' out of respect for this ineffable name" (*ST* 2–2.174.6). Thus the same statement that guarantees that God exists and that his most suitable name is He Who Is, also reveals to us the perfect simplicity of the divine essence. And indeed, God did not say: I am this or that, but simply I Am. I am what? I am 'I Am.' So, more than ever, the statement of Exodus seems to soar above in a kind of empty space, where the attraction of the weight of philosophy can no longer be felt. The work of reason is good, healthy, and important, for it proves that, left to itself, philosophy can establish with certitude the existence of the primary being whom everyone calls God. But a single word of the sacred text at once puts us in personal relations with him. We say his name, and by the simple fact of saying it, it teaches us the simplicity of the divine essence.

If we reflect on the significance of this last remark, it will make us even more aware of the absolute transcendence of a science such as theology, and in what sense it is true to say that natural reason, which it makes its servant, never empties it of faith.

5. Meditate on *ST* 2–2.2.3 and ad 3m.

2

The Cause of Being

Ex ipso et per ipsum et in ipso sunt omnia (Romans 11:36).[1]

Many Thomists find great consolation in the thought that St. Thomas himself was an Aristotelian philosopher, or, if you prefer, that he was an Aristotelian insofar as he was a philosopher. It would be wrong to contradict them, for it seems as hard to refute this assertion as it is to prove it. The concept "Aristotelian" is too imprecise for two dialecticians to be able to contradict each other about it. The same remark applies to the concepts "Cartesian," "Kantian" or "Hegelian."

There would be no reason to bring up this question if in fact it did not depend on another whose solution seems to be taken for granted. Why hesitate to answer "no" to the question: Was St. Thomas an Aristotelian? My point is, why do those who refuse to answer "yes" often hesitate at the moment of answering "no"? It is because the writings of St. Thomas clearly draw upon the thought of Aristotle, his philosophical technique, method, philosophy of nature, ethics, and metaphysics. So it is said that if St. Thomas had wanted to have a philosophy as independent of all religious revelation as those of the ancient philosophers, he would have chosen that of Aristotle. And there is no objection to this, except that, if St.Thomas had done this, there would only have been one more Aristotelian. We would not have a Thomist philosophy.

It is fortunate for us that St. Thomas did something completely different. There is nothing that we know of his life, his studies, and his writings that would lead us to think that he was ever thought to be a philosopher or that he aspired to have a per-

1. ["For from him and through him and in him are all things."]

sonal philosophy. For a theologian who has climbed to the summit, that would have been to want to descend and to set his heart on something lower. It is only since the sixteenth century that the specific development of philosophical studies needed by future theologians led to the division of religious studies into two parts: scholastic philosophy and scholastic theology. From this time on, whatever philosophy was included in scholastic theologies, or explicitly elaborated in view of these theologies and for their use, was set up as a distinct body of doctrine. This is what the thirteenth-century Averroists and their followers had already done, but they intended not only to distinguish between the two disciplines but to separate them. Scholastics from the sixteenth century to the present have cherished a sort of dream: to construct as a preamble to theology a philosophy that would owe nothing to it except a kind of external control, and that nevertheless would be in perfect harmony with it. Modern scholastics, being Thomists almost by definition (although there are numerous exceptions), naturally want this philosophy to be St. Thomas's – which presupposes that St. Thomas had a philosophy. So they attribute Aristotle's to him, touched up, however, as we are assured the Philosopher himself would have been able to do in order to make it agree with Christian theology.

There can be different opinions whether it is advisable to adopt this attitude. What is very difficult to accept is the transference of this way of thinking to the past and the pretension that it was already that of St. Thomas. It is of less importance, however, whether or not we attribute to him a philosophy properly so-called, provided at least that the one ascribed to him agrees with the philosophical theses he himself explicitly taught in his theological writings, chiefly in the two Summas and the Disputed Questions. It is beyond dispute that the influence of Aristotle's philosophy on the theology of St. Thomas far outweighs that of other philosophers. It is preponderant in the sense that, having to summon philosophy for the service of theology, St. Thomas chiefly used Aristotle's; but what he made Aristotle say is always what he ought to say in order to serve the purposes of the theologian. And he is not the only one to serve them.

The theology of St. Thomas is changed if one imagines that it could have been linked to any philosophical doctrine whatsoever, even if it were the one the theologian judged by far to be the best of all. When St. Thomas reflects on what human reason can know about God by its own powers, without the help of the Judeo-Christian revelation, he raises the problem, not from the point of view of Aristotle alone, but in connection with the whole history of Greek philosophy; for in his eyes this comprised the entire history of philosophy, the period that followed having been little more than that of the commentators and saints.

St. Thomas has sketched a general picture of this history several times. As he knew and interpreted it, it appeared to be governed by a general rule: God can be discovered only as the cause of beings given in sensible experience, and the idea that reason forms of him is more elevated to the extent that it has a deeper knowledge of the nature of his effects. In other words, we cannot discover a God more perfect than the one we are looking for. In order to find the most perfect God that it is capable of conceiving by its unaided powers, natural reason must investigate the cause of what is most perfect in sensible beings such as it knows them.

Under the theologian's scrutiny, this history appears as a progression that is not continuous but without retrogressions, and marked out by a small number of definite stages. The progress in deepening insight into the nature of beings which goes along with that of our knowledge of God follows a definite order, which is that of human knowledge: *secundum ordinem cognitionis humanae processerunt antiqui in consideratione naturae rerum* (The ancients progressed in the study of the nature of things following the order of human knowledge: QDP 3.5). Now our knowledge begins with sensible things, and from them it progressively rises to the intelligible by a series of ever-deepening abstractions.

The first stage corresponds to the sensible perception of the qualities of bodies. So it was natural for the first philosophers to be materialists, for the simple reason that at the start they mistook reality for what they could perceive of it with the senses. Modern materialists ("I only believe in what I can see or touch") are simply philosophers who have not gone beyond the first stage of the philosophical history of the human mind. For them, substance is matter. They do not even conceive it as endowed with a substantial form, for substantial forms are not perceptible to the senses. On the contrary, the qualities of bodies, which are accidental forms, can be perceived by the five senses.

According to the first philosophers, then, reality consisted of matter, which is substance, and accidents, which are caused by the constitutive principles of material substance or elements. They needed nothing else in order to explain the appearances of the sensible world. Let us clearly understand this position as St. Thomas himself did. If we posit matter as a substance whose elements suffice to account for all the sensible qualities of bodies, the latter are nothing else than the appearance of these qualities. Accordingly they do not have to be produced; they are present simply because material substance, of which they are accidental forms, is present. Hence the important conclusion that, for those who espouse a philosophy of this sort, matter is the ultimate cause of all appearances. So there is no need to posit a cause of matter, or, more exactly, these philosophers are compelled to say that matter has no cause, and this, for St. Thomas, amounts to a complete denial of efficient causality: *unde ponere cogebantur materiae causam non esse, et negare totaliter causam efficientem.*

This last remark is of great significance. To say that matter has no cause is "a complete denial of efficient causality." It seems that here, as so often happens with St. Thomas, he puts a bit of dynamite in our hands, while leaving to our discretion how we are to use it. At the same time we see why, for as soon as we continue our reflection, we find ourselves caught up in a series of far-reaching consequences. Keeping as close as possible to the text of *De potentia* 3.5, on which we are reflecting, the meaning of the position he is discussing is simple. The only substance is matter, which is the cause of all its accidents, and there is no other cause. Nothing could be clearer. But from this how does it follow that the position amounts to "a complete denial of efficient causality"?

It seems that we have to reconstruct the reasoning of which this is but an abbreviated form – a delicate operation for which the interpreter alone must bear the responsibility. It must be done, however, if we want to understand it. We propose the following: The only actual being accidents have is that of their substance. Hence the production of accidents by substance is not a production of being (otherwise the being of the substance would produce itself). On the other hand, in a materialist philosophy, material substance has no efficient cause because it is the primary being. Thus, neither substance nor accidents have an efficient cause, from which it follows that there is no efficient cause at all.

If this is indeed the meaning of the reasoning, its conclusion is that efficient causality cannot be found in a universe in which the only substance is *an uncreated matter*. But it does not follow from this that there cannot be an efficient cause in an uncreated universe. There can be one, provided that substance is not reduced to matter. Nevertheless, even then there remains something in such a universe that will always escape causal knowledge, namely matter itself, whose existence has no explanation, though it itself explains everything else. We could not wish for a stronger affirmation of the primacy of efficient causality in the order of being.

The second stage was reached by later philosophers who began to some extent to take substantial forms into consideration. Since these forms are invisible, by so doing they rose from sensible knowledge to intellectual knowledge. This was a definite progress, for, by moving from the sensible to the intellectual order they reached the universal. Nevertheless, this second family of philosophers did not inquire if there were universal forms and universal causes; they centered all their attention on forms of certain species. Now it was a question of truly agent causes (*aliquas causas agentes*), but causes that did not give being to things, in the sense in which this word applies universally to everything that is. The substantial forms in question only changed matter by impressing on it now one form, now another. This was how Anaxagoras explained the diversity of certain substantial forms by appealing to the Intelligence, or how Empedocles explained them by Love and Hate. There still remained something unaccounted for in these doctrines, for agent causes of this sort explained well enough how matter passed from one form to another, but "even according to these philosophers, all beings did not come from an efficient cause. Matter was presupposed to the action of the agent cause." The primacy of the efficient cause stands out ever more clearly, as is fitting in an article treating of the question whether there can exist something that has not been created by God. But, as a matter of fact, we have the impression that, for St. Thomas, the creative act is as it were the archetype and perfect model of efficient causality. We do not wish to make his language stricter than he himself does, but perhaps it is not out of place to point out that here St. Thomas prefers to reserve the term *causa agens* to the formal cause, whose effect is to produce being of such and such a nature in a given matter, and the term *causa efficiens* to that whose efficacy would extend to matter itself: *et ideo etiam secundum ipsos non omnia entia a* causa efficiente *procedebant, sed materia actioni* causae agentis *praesupponebatur* (and therefore, even in their view, all beings did not come forth from an *efficient cause,* but matter was presupposed to the action of an *agent cause: QDP* 3.5).

The final stage was reached by another group of philosophers, such as Plato, Aristotle, and their schools. Having succeeded in taking into account being itself in all its universality, they alone posited a universal cause of things on which everything else depended for its being. St. Thomas, whom we are trying to follow literally in all this, directs us here to St. Augustine's *De civitate Dei* 8.4;[2] but what is important is that our theologian would place in one and the same group philosophers like Plato and Aristotle, even though the latter often contradicted the former. The remark also applies to those who afterward formed their schools (*Plato, Aristoteles et eorum sequaces*), for among the followers of Aristotle whom he must have had in mind are Avicenna and Averroes, whose numerous disagreements are well known. But this is of little importance here, for the point at issue is whether there can exist something that is not *created* by God. So all the philosophers who posited some sort of *universal cause* of things (*aliquam universalem causam rerum*) are unanimous in supporting the theological conclusion that there is no being that is not created by God. This is the teaching of the Catholic faith itself, but it can be proved by three arguments. Here we have a striking example of the transcendence of theological wisdom and a priceless lesson for those who want to understand the very liberal and complex attitude of St. Thomas with regard to philosophies, including Aristotle's as well as Plato's.

The first philosophical reason for affirming a cause of universal being that St. Thomas appeals to here is based on the principle that, when one thing is found in common in several beings, a single cause must be responsible for its presence in them. Indeed, the presence in common of the same thing in several different beings can be explained neither by their differences nor by a number of

2. [*De civitate Dei* 8.4, ed. Bernard Dombart and Alphonse Kalb CCL 47: 219–221.]

different causes. Now, being (*esse*) belongs in common to all things, for they are alike in that *they are*, though they differ from each other in *what they are*. So it necessarily follows that they do not possess their being from themselves but from one single cause. Note the invaluable precision St. Thomas brings to his own thought: "This seems to be Plato's argument, who required that a unity precede every plurality, not only in numbers but even in the nature of things" (*QDP* 3.5).

The second argument is taken from the degrees of being and perfection. The first simply affirmed the one as the cause of the many; this argument affirms the absolute, or the supreme degree in every genus, as the cause of everything that differs more or less within the same genus. It is the degree of participation in a genus that demands the affirmation in the genus of a supreme term, the single cause of its unequal participations. We immediately recall the *quarta via* of the *Summa theologiae* (1.2.3), but with a remarkable modification. In the *Summa* the fourth way leads directly to the existence of God, for if there are beings that are more or less beings, there must be a supreme being that is the cause of the being and all the perfections of all other beings. In the article of the *De potentia* (3.5) that we are following here, the final conclusion is different: "But it is necessary to posit a single being that is the most perfect and most true being. This is proved by the fact that there is an entirely immobile and most perfect mover, as the philosophers have proved. Hence everything less perfect than it possesses its being from it." Here the *prima via* comes to reinforce the *quarta via* of the *Summa* and brings it to its conclusion.

We should pay close attention to the limits of the services St. Thomas expects here from the philosophers. It is enough for his purpose that both Plato and Aristotle rose to the consideration of universal being and that they assigned a single cause to it. More exactly, it is enough for St. Thomas that these philosophers had the wisdom to assign a single cause to one of the transcendental properties of being as being, whether it was unity for Plato or goodness and perfection for Aristotle. These properties are universal attributes of being, and St. Thomas honors these philosophers for having concluded that they must necessarily have a single cause, but he does not ascribe to either of them a metaphysics of creation. Plato and Aristotle explain everything about being except its very existence.

The third argument leads us as close to existence as the philosophers have ever approached it. It is the following: What exists by another is reduced to what exists by itself as to its cause. Now the beings given in experience are not purely and simply being. We cannot simply say of any one of them: it *is*. We must always say: it is this or that. We shall have to return to this important fact. For the present it will suffice to recall that there does not exist any simple being (that is, simply and solely being) that is given in experience.

What is only a certain way of being, or a being of a certain species, is clearly only a certain way of participating being, and the limits of its participation are determined by the definition of its species. If there are beings by way of participation, there must first be a being in itself: *est ponere aliquod ens quod est ipsum suum esse*, that is, a first being which is the pure act of being and nothing else. Hence it is necessary, St. Thomas concludes, "that it is through this single being that all other things exist which *are* not their being but *have* being by way of participation." He then adds, "This is the argument of Avicenna."[3]

There are few articles of St. Thomas that enable us to see more clearly how he understood the work of the theologian. He himself does not need a proof in order to know that everything that exists has been created by God. Faith suffices for him to be sure of it. The *sed contra* of his article, which he takes from the Epistle to the Romans 11:36, is a reminder of this: "Everything is *from* him *through* him and *in* him." But theology, as he understands it, seeks to join to the certitude of faith rational certitudes whose purpose is to prepare the mind to receive it; or, if it has already received it, to give the mind *some* understanding of it. In any case, it is not a question of pretending that the philosophers have reached precisely the object to which faith gives its assent. But the conclusions of reason and the certitudes of faith are in agreement and harmony, to such a degree that the development of problems in the course of history shows us that progress in philosophy's way of raising and resolving them gradually approaches

3. [Avicenna, *Liber de philosophia prima sive scientia divina* 8.7 and 9.4, ed. S. Van Riet, 2 vols. (Louvain: Peeters; Leiden: Brill, 1977–1980), 2: 423–433, 476–488.]

the meaning of the truths of faith. In the end, if it does not reach these truths, it has a presentiment of them.

At the same time this shows us how difficult it is to tie the thought of St. Thomas to one single philosophy. Plato, Aristotle, Avicenna are three different philosophers, and without wishing to deny that their philosophies are connected, they are certainly not the same. It is impossible to hold the three philosophies at the same time, as if a metaphysics of the One could at the same time be a metaphysics of Substance and a metaphysics of Necessary Being. There could not be three equally primary principles. Nevertheless, we have just seen St. Thomas call to witness these three metaphysics to show how "it is proved by reason and held on faith that everything is created by God." How are we to understand this way of philosophizing?

To those who accuse it of philosophical incoherence, some reply that Thomism is an eclecticism, but this acknowledges the incoherence with which its opponents reproach it. Like every being, a philosophy must be *one* in order *to be*. A philosophy is not one if it is made up of pieces borrowed from different philosophies and more or less skilfully sewn together. Each of these pieces takes its meaning from the whole philosophy from which it is extracted; so it could not unite with other pieces taken from philosophies with different meanings. The unity of a doctrine is not necessarily inflexible; it can take its riches wherever it finds them, provided they are truly *its* riches. The unity of a philosophy, and consequently its existence, is recognized by the presence of a kind of intelligible thread, a golden thread, that runs through it in all directions and from within binds together all its parts. Philosophers worthy of the name are not rhapsodists, sewers, bone-setters.

In reply, it can be said that the doctrine of St. Thomas is not a philosophical but a theological eclecticism. The expression would be more satisfactory if it were not contradictory. A doctrine whose elements are the result of a theological choice is necessarily a theology. Wherever it is present and active, theology rules. Besides, if the theologian who made the choice were content to sew together again the pieces such as they are, from which he claims to fashion a philosophy, it would suffer from the lack of unity and being endemic to all eclecticisms and, to make matters worse, the principle governing the choice of pieces would no longer be philosophical and strictly rational.

The attitude of the theologian is profoundly different. He does not resort to the light of faith in order to create a philosophy that would have unity, but rather, in order to proceed to a critique of the philosophies he will use to create a body of theology that would have unity. What is in question here is not the unity of faith but the structural unity of the theology as a science. In this regard it is very true that St. Thomas's debt to Aristotle exceeds by far what he owes to any other philosophy, perhaps even to all other philosophies combined; but it is none the less true that, as a theologian, the sole object of his endeavor is to establish a theology, not a philosophy. Whatever philosophical unity the doctrine thus created will have will come to it from a light higher than that of philosophy. The reason it can use several without risking incoherence is that it is not tied to any one of them, that it does not depend on any one of them, and that it first transforms whatever it seems to borrow from them.

Nothing can take the place of a personal meditation on a text like that of *De potentia* 3.5 (but there are many others), in order to come in real contact with the practice of the theologian and to appreciate the nature of his work. St. Thomas reveals himself there to be neither a Platonist, an Aristotelian, nor an Avicennian. If we delve deeply into these three philosophies, we see that no one of them conceived the notion of creation *ex nihilo*, including the creation of matter. But as they bathe here in the light of theology, we see them reveal richer philosophical possibilities than they seemed to have in the minds of the philosophers who first conceived them. The meaning of the five ways to the existence of God, the meaning of the three arguments for the universal causality of the primary being, in the last resort do not originate in any of these ways or arguments.

Their source is a definite notion of God and being whose light, shining from a mind impregnated by faith, suffices to transform the philosophies it touches. But these matters can be appreciated only with the experience that comes from long study. Virtuosity in dialectics, rather than making their demonstration possible, stands in the way of demonstrating them well.

3

He Who Is

Dei igitur essentia est suum esse. Hanc autem sublimem veritatem Moyses a Domino est edoctus, qui, cum quae-reret a Domino, dicens: *Si dixerint ad me filii Israel: Quod est nomen ejus? quid dicam eis? Dominus respondit: Ego sum qui sum; sic dices filiis Israel: Qui est misit me ad vos* [Exodus 3:13–14], ostendens suum proprium nomen esse: *Qui est (Summa contra Gentiles* 1.22.9–10).[1]

St. Thomas himself did not succeed in condensing in one single truth the whole content of these words of Exodus. Or rather, it is we who are unable to see at once all their aspects. When he says, *Ego sum qui sum*, God affirms his own existence as God. He does not say: Know that there is a God, but rather: Know that I am, and that my name is He Who Is. So that the people of Israel would not think that he is a new God still unknown to them, the revelation continues: "Say this to the children of Israel: Yahweh, the God of your fathers, the God of Abraham, the God of Isaac, and the God of Jacob, has sent me to you. This is my name for-ever, and thus I am to be invoked for all future generations" (Exod. 3:15).

Thus, as was said above,[2] God reveals his name along with his existence, and because in the same statement in a way he reveals his essence, he thereby says – if we follow the inter-pretations of St. Thomas – both that the divine essence is simple (*ST* 1.3.7) and that the essence of God is his being: *Dei … essentia*

1. ["Therefore the essence of God is his being. The Lord taught Moses this sublime truth when he asked the Lord: *If the children of Israel ask me what is his name? what shall I say to them? The Lord replied: I am who am … say this to the children of Israel: He Who Is has sent me to you,* showing that his proper name is *He who is.*"]

2. See above p. 12.

est suum esse (CG 1.22.9). Let us try to make our way through this maze of ideas.

At the outset we must take the occasion that presents itself to express respect and admiration for, and gratitude to, the excellent family of philologists.[3] Armed with their grammars and dictionaries, supported by their methods which they regard as "scientific," they think themselves qualified to give a correct interpretation of the sacred text. We would not deny their competence, provided that it recognizes its own limitations. Philology allows one to establish the meaning of a text with the utmost precision, provided that the writer was a person like others, with a mentality like ours, using the language of contemporary society in order to express ideas similar to those which it signified by the same words.

The method can be applied to scripture, but only on the supposition that we lay down in principle not only that the sacred writer was a person like others, but, besides, that he was absolutely nothing more than that. If we do this, the notion of an inspired author vanishes and scripture becomes in fact a book like the *Iliad* or the *Aeneid*, entirely amenable to philology and the philologists. Even then there would be reason to be on guard, for the meaning of texts is in neither grammars nor dictionaries, but in the mind of the reader who translates or interprets them. Above all (and this is our only concern), no philological science could tell us the meaning an inspired author gave to his words, for the sacred writer is by definition a person who tries to utter truths beyond human comprehension. He must use words that everyone else does in order to express thoughts that are not those of everyone else. For the philologist, the words of the Pentateuch have the meaning they would have had in the mouth of anyone speaking about a topic of conversation familiar to his contemporaries. To depend on the probable meaning of the same words in other passages of the Bible is to presuppose that in no case and at no moment has the sacred writer wanted to utter a word with

---

3. [See Gilson, "Yahweh et les grammairiens," in his *Constantes philosophiques de l'être*, avant-propos de Jean-François Courtine, Bibliothèque des textes philosophiques (Paris: Vrin, 1983), pp. 231–253.]

a unique meaning whose equivalent would be impossible to find anywhere else.

But this is not what is most serious. It is enough to see into what contradictions the philologists are apt to fall and in what bitter disputes they engage, not to let oneself be taken in by the apparent certitude of their conclusions. The methods of philology are shaky enough to leave room for arbitrariness, and in the end they allow the exegete to make the text say what he wants it to say. It is not surprising that biblical exegesis described as scientific is held in respect especially in Protestant churches. It is a scholarly form of free inquiry, in which the alleged objectivity and necessity of the conclusions are the guarantee that revealed truths can no longer depend on the magisterium of the Church and tradition. The philologists' methods of exegesis are necessary, but their claim to be sufficient is intolerable. They must not be allowed to make us believe that meanings – even literal ones – that are beyond their reach, are meanings that do not exist.

A Catholic at least could not be satisfied with methods of this sort. Scripture is given to him replete with all the meanings with which it is charged through the centuries and which it has inherited through tradition. Clearly, no philologist, speaking as such, could agree with this, but precisely, philology is not theology, and it makes no sense to claim that a method designed for literary texts of the contemporary kind can extract for us the supernatural meaning contained in a revealed text.

The Church is best qualified to settle the literal sense or senses the sacred author had in mind while writing. This is not a philological method, but the Catholic believes that scripture is a book written under the inspiration of the Holy Spirit. It is no wonder, then, that it raises insoluble problems for the interpreter whose only instruments are grammar and a dictionary. The Catholic sees no impossibility in the inspired texts truly and really containing meanings unknown to those who wrote them, but which divine inspiration has in a way given them for the future. The statement of St. Thomas must be taken literally: *auctor sacrae scripturae est Deus* (God is the author of sacred scripture). No doubt the writings of an author who is also extraordinary do not surrender all their meaning to one who limits himself to the usual methods of the exegesis of texts. Indeed, "The literal sense is the one the author has in his mind; and since the author of sacred scripture is God, whose intellect comprehends everything at once, it is not impossible, as Augustine says in the *Confessions*, book 12,[4] that even regarding the literal sense, one and the same passage of scripture have several meanings" (*ST* 1.1.10). So the text of Exodus can by itself contain in the literal sense everything that the Fathers of the Church have read in it, and everything St. Thomas just read in it.[5]

The fundamental certainty that God is the author of scripture, and that he speaks to us in the sacred text with his own knowledge, explains the perfect ease with which St. Thomas reads in it the most abstruse metaphysical speculations. His exegesis is that of a theologian who has mastered all the resources of natural theology – the human science of divine things – and who strives to make natural reason speak the greatest possible amount of truth within the bosom, so to speak, of revealed truth. The often-expressed fear that reason lets itself be corrupted by faith is pointless on two scores. First, the theologian is not at all concerned to enlist the services of a philosophy that is unfaithful to its own methods and hence could no longer be of any help to him. On the other hand, the theologian does not think for a moment that his work can consist in changing revealed truth into the truth of philosophy. That idea would horrify him. The *fides quaerens intellectum* is a faith that remains irreducibly faith, as long as it has not vanished before the beatific vision. The *intellectus fidei* is an understanding of an intelligible object proposed by revelation; but what the intellect understands, precious as it may be, in no way penetrates the supernatural reality whose substance is the very object that faith obscurely possesses.

Accordingly we should not think of the theology of the preambles of faith as though it were a sort of philosophical introduc-

4. [*Confessions* 12.31 (42), ed. Lucas Verheijen CCL 27: 240–241.]

5. The explanation of Exodus 3.13–14 in the Jerusalem Bible shows how the most correct philosophy can be in harmony with St. Thomas's rule of theological interpretation. No interpretation is acceptable if the literal sense cannot bear it; but if God is its author, one and the same statement can have several literal meanings. [See *The Jerusalem Bible*, ed. Alexander Jones et al. (Garden City, New York: Doubleday, 1966), p. 81, note h.]

tion, or a preface written in the style of metaphysics, awaiting the
true beginning of theological speculation. Theology begins with
the first *sed contra* of the *Summa*, and all the philosophical speculation the latter contains is integrated into theology in whose service the theologian employs it. It cannot be of service unless it is
truly philosophy; but the servant belongs to the family; she is part
of the household.

It is a fatal mistake to lose sight of this truth when approach-
ing the third question of the *Summa*. You can still believe you are
keeping it in mind, but you are lost. No sooner has St. Thomas
proved the existence of God in the two *Summae* than he undertakes to establish his perfect simplicity. But we have no experience
of any real being that is not a composite. We cannot imagine a
perfectly simple being, because nature does not provide us with
an example of one. To establish that God is simple, is accordingly
to establish that God *is not* in the way composite beings *are*. The
proof of the divine simplicity is the first instance we shall meet of
the use of the negative method in theology. What is in question
is knowing about God *quomodo non sit* (*ST* 1.3, div. text.), and to
this end to remove all composition from the notion we form of
him.

This operation is carried out according to a well-known dialectical progression, each stage of which consists in demonstrating
a particular *God is not composed of* ...: God is not composed of
movable and hence material parts; he is not composed of form
and matter, and so on, until finally, when even the least trace of
composition has been excluded from the notion of God, the mind
is compelled to affirm his perfect simplicity. Nothing is easier than
to follow step by step the progress of this demonstration, which
is completely rational and only employs notions familiar to
traditional Aristotelianism. Act and potency, form and matter,
supposit and nature, finally essence and being – nothing of all
this comes from revelation.

Nevertheless, this dialectic, which is rational and properly
philosophical in structure, is developed in light of a statement of
God which directs it, guides it, and leads it finally to its goal.
What statement? The *sed contra* of the question "Does God exist?"
(*ST* 1.2.3), which, as we recall, is *Ego sum qui sum*. We cannot
grasp the entire beginning of the *Summa*, or consequently correctly interpret what follows, if for a single moment we lose sight

of God's revelation of his existence and the name under which he revealed himself. We must try to place this dialectical progression in its true perspective if we are not to lose its meaning.

This can be demonstrated. Proving the simplicity of God amounts to proving the simplicity of his being. In other words, the process consists in proving that in this unique case the being of God is precisely that which he is. This means that the process primarily depends on the notion of the divine being that it presupposes; and since God is being *par excellence*, the notion of the divine simplicity will depend, for the theologian, on the particular ontology that he will accept as a philosopher. Indeed, even if it be granted that God is purely and simply being, we still have to know what being itself is.

The meaning of this remark will be apparent if we turn directly to the article in which St. Thomas's dialectical progression culminates: "Are essence and being one and the same in God?" (*ST* 1.3.4). To raise the question is implicitly to assume that being an essence is not identical with being a being; or, vice versa, that being is not identical with being an essence. Many theologians and philosophers would not even think of raising the question. At the moment when he asks it, St. Thomas himself just established that, considered as a supposit or subject, God is identical with his own essence or nature. If a being and its essence are identical; if, in other words, a being is identical with what it is, how is it possible to conceive it as being even more simple? There is nothing more simple than self-identity.

Clearly, the theologian who here transcends the order of essence to reach that of the act of being is the same as the philosopher of the *De ente et essentia*. He knows that in a being (*ens*) the essence does not contain anything to account for its being (*esse*). On the contrary, actual being (*esse*) is the actuality of every form or nature, for a man is a man only on condition that he exists. What *is not* is nothing. In order to prove that God is simple, then, it is not enough to establish that God is identical with his essence. In order to remove all composition from him, we must reduce his notion to what is absolutely last in a being, namely *esse*, the act through which it *is*, simply and ultimately.

But why would the act of being be absolutely last? Why not stop the dialectical progression at essence rather than at existence? If the being and essence of God are identical, it should be possible to affirm that God is the highest, absolute, and simple essence, and to reduce the divine existence to it, instead of reducing the essence to it. No matter how we view the final moment of this progress toward the simplicity of being, we find something arbitrary in the theologian's decision to bring it to its ultimate conclusion, not in the essence of a being, but in the very act of existing.

This is because the reader of the *Summa*, who of course is paying attention to the dialectic of being he is invited to follow, is once again tempted to think that St. Thomas mounts from philosophy to theology, whereas in fact he does the opposite. No doubt there are many reasons for thinking that there is in beings a composition of essence and being, but no one of them strictly demonstrates it. It is evident, or demonstrable, that a finite being does not have its being from itself. A finite essence, therefore, is in potency to its actual being, and this composition of potency and act suffices to distinguish radically the being which is only *a being*, from him who is Being. But how is it possible to demonstrate, by directly examining a being, that its actual existence is the effect of a finite act within its substance making it a being (*ens*), in the precise sense of an essence having its own act of existing? Duns Scotus, Suárez, and countless other theologians have refused, and still refuse, to accept this metaphysical doctrine.

Perhaps not enough thought is given to the serious theological consequence of this refusal. If a real finite substance is not composed of essence and being, there is no longer a reason to eliminate this composition from our notion of God in order to establish his perfect simplicity. The undertaking becomes pointless, for we cannot eliminate from the divine being a composition that exists nowhere except in the mind of those who conceive it. So the theologian follows the opposite procedure. Knowing that God's proper name is 'Is,'[6] because he has said so, the theologian holds that a finite being is necessarily complex. Now, he begins with God as absolutely simple. Therefore the complexity of a finite substance must result in the first place from an addition to the basic act of being. That primary addition can only be that of an

6. [This is an echo of Augustine; see below p. 61 and n9, and p. 73 and n18.]

essence, through which an act of being is that of a particular being. If the act of being (*actus essendi, esse*) were not a real metaphysical component of a being, it would not make a real composition with the essence. A being would be simple like the divine being; it would be God.

The certainty that *esse*, or the act of being, is properly speaking an element of a being, and therefore included in its structure, is explained first of all by the prior certainty that the act of being actually exists in and by itself, in the absolute metaphysical purity of what *has* nothing, not even essence, because it *is* everything that we could wish to attribute to it. Whereas He Who Is excludes all addition, a finite substance is necessarily composed of an act of being and of that which limits it. It is because it is known that God is pure being that the metaphysical core of reality is located in a metaphysical non-pure act of being.

This whole dialectic is set in motion, directed and concluded in the light of the word of Exodus. It is metaphysical in its method and structure, for nothing in the sacred text either suggests it or proclaims it. Revelation as such can fulfill its own purpose without having recourse to it, and it must be admitted that humanly speaking the primitive literal sense of scripture would not suggest any technical Aristotelian procedure. Nevertheless, St. Thomas read in it at once and indivisibly that God exists, that he is Being, and that he is simple. Now, to be He Who Is and to be simple is properly speaking *to be*, purely and simply. St. Thomas showed a remarkable intellectual boldness in leading the philosophical dialectic of being, which would halt spontaneously at substance and essence, to the point it had to go in order to join the truth of the divine word. Since God has revealed himself as He Who Is, the philosopher knows that at the origin and very heart of beings it is necessary to place the pure act of existing. The divine word absolutely transcends the philosophical notions conceived in its light; that is also why they could not be deduced from it. We do not say: Since scripture says so, the philosophical notions of being and God are in the last analysis identical with that of the act of being. In fact, scripture itself does not say this; but it does say that the proper name of God is He Who Is. Because it says this I believe it. While I thus cling to the object of faith, the intellect, made fruitful by this contact, makes deeper progress in the understanding of the primary notion of being.

With one and the same movement it discovers an unforeseen depth in the philosophical meaning of the first principle and gains a kind of imperfect but true knowledge of the object of faith.

It is this very movement that is called Christian philosophy, for the modest, though invaluable understanding of the word of God that it brings with it. It receives the name scholastic philosophy for the doctrinal order, the broadenings of perspective, and the deepening of philosophical views that the movement brings about. Under both these complementary aspects it is inseparable from scripture. Accordingly, we should strive at length, or better yet, frequently, either to become aware of the presence of a dialectic of the divine simplicity in the fullness of the divine name, or inversely, at our leisure to unfold this dialectic in the light of *Ego sum qui sum.*

4

Beyond Essence

> Sed secundum rei veritatem causa prima est supra ens, in
> quantum est ipsum esse infinitum, ens autem dicitur id
> quod finite participat esse, et hoc est proportionatum
> intellectui nostro cujus objectum est quod quid est, ut
> dicitur in III° *De anima.* Unde illud solum est capabile ab
> intellectu nostro quod habet quidditatem participantem
> esse; sed Dei quidditas est ipsum esse, unde est supra
> intellectum (*Expositio super librum 'De causis'* prop. 6).[1]

God is being. Scripture says so, or at least it is often claimed that
scripture says so. But if God is He Who Is, his *esse* takes the place
of essence; and, as every being is an essence endowed with an
existence, the notion of a being does not properly belong to God.
Like the Good of Plato, God must be placed beyond a being: *causa
prima est supra ens.*

No one pays more attention to the habits of thought and
language than St. Thomas. He does not directly go counter to
them, and never unnecessarily, but we should be all the more
careful to collect the all-important words in which his language,
which is so precise, sometimes embraces everything he holds to be
absolutely true about a subject.

---

1. ["But in truth the first cause transcends a being inasmuch as he
is infinite being. A being is said to be that which participates being in
a limited way; and this is proportionate to our intellect, whose object
is essence, as is said in *De anima* (3.4, 429b10). So our intellect can only
grasp that which has a quiddity participating in being. But the
quiddity of God is being itself. Hence he transcends the intellect"
(Aquinas, *Expositio super librum 'De causis,'* ed. H.D. Saffrey, Textus philosophici friburgenses 4/5 [Freiburg: Société philosophique; Louvain:
Nauwelaerts, 1954], p. 47.11–18).]

Such is the present case. We are free to say, and we ourselves do say, that God is *ens*. We shall see presently why this is allowed. Nevertheless, we should not forget that in the last analysis the true name of God is not *ens* but *esse*. If the day should come when the French language allowed it, this truth will be expressed by saying that God is not an *étant* (*ens*) but an *être* (*esse*). Since French usage unfortunately does not yet permit us to do this, we should at least make it a point never to conceive God as what we ordinarily call *a being*. We just recalled that in the proper sense of the words *ens* (or *étant*), a being is something possessing actual existence, that is, *esse* or *actus essendi*. This something, the subject that receives the act of being (*esse*), is called essence. As a consequence, since every being except God is composed of an act of being limited by an essence, it is finite by definition. On the other hand, since God is the pure act of being, *esse* itself (*ipsum esse*), without any essence limiting it, he is infinite by his very notion. If every being, then, is finite inasmuch as it *has* the act of existing but *is* not it, it amounts to the same thing to say that God is, that he is He Who Is, that he is perfectly simple, that he is infinite, and situated beyond *ens*. God is infinite because his simplicity is that of the pure act of *esse*, which is neither this nor that but *is* absolutely.

The word of Exodus is here enriched with a new dimension. Strictly speaking, this consists rather in ascribing to it a dimension incommensurable with any other, or more simply in refusing to limit it by any dimension. And it is for this reason that, having observed that God is even above a being (*ens*), whose notion implies finiteness (*habens esse*), St. Thomas will nevertheless allow us to say that God is first in the order of being and supremely being (*maxime ens*). It is because we ourselves are composed of essence and *esse*, that the fitting object of the human intellect is not pure *esse* but a being (*ens*), which we have just said is always an act of existing determined and limited by an essence. If such is its proper object, our intellect cannot conceive objects of a different kind. Material objects are below it. They evade it by the singularity of their material determinations. Pure existence is above it, surpassing the human intellect by the infinity of its act. It only remains to draw from these premises the consequence they imply. Our intellect is only able to grasp what has a quiddity or essence participating in existence (*esse*). Now the quiddity of God is existence itself (*ipsum esse*). Hence he is above the intellect.

We shall never meditate too long on this truth. Admittedly it disturbs some good souls who find a touch of agnosticism in it, but even though the criticism is baseless, the truth of authentic Thomism would be ill-served by concealing the doctrine to avoid the objection. On the contrary, we discover both its meaning and its justification by probing the doctrine to its depths and by expressing it in all its rigor.

The human mind knows and expresses many truths about what is usually called "the divine nature." In more technical language we would say that we can form true affirmative propositions about God. Every created perfection can rightly be affirmed of the creator, and affirmations of this sort are based on reality. There is no temptation to pragmatism in the thought of St. Thomas. When the Christian says "Our Father ..." he does not think that God deals with us as a father. Neither does he think naively that on our part our attitude toward God should be animated by the feelings of a son for his father. We love God as a father because he *is* our father. The whole reality of fatherhood is truly in him, or rather, is him. It is the same with the other perfections of finite being that we attribute to the first cause. We validly predicate of God words like justice, truth and goodness and what they signify. The reason for this is simple. There is nothing existing that God is not first of all as its cause. So there is no name signifying a perfection that is not by prior right applicable to God. The cause of all perfections rightfully bears their names, for it is them.

Nevertheless we must go beyond this point of view if we want to think of God as St. Thomas did. The natural object of the human mind is the quiddity abstracted from sensible experience. Since this fact is bound up with human nature itself, the substantial unity of a soul and a body, it allows for no exceptions. No concept, whatever its object and degree of abstraction may be, including even the concept of being itself, contains anything else than a quiddity, essence or nature belonging to material things perceptible to the senses. Images, without which we cannot conceive anything, are the signs of the sensible origin of all the abstract notions our intellect conceives.

The first consequence of this principle is among those most difficult to grasp and to weigh its exact meaning. We have the notions of created perfections which, because they come from God, are truly in him. If he were not at least what they are, how could God cause them? On the other hand, God is immaterial and simple, and since we can only represent created perfections in the form in which they present themselves in sensible experience, God cannot in any way be represented to us. God truly is what we call in our language good, beautiful, true, powerful, knowing, loving, and so forth. But when the mind forms these abstract notions in order to ascribe them to God, there are always images of good, beautiful, powerful, knowing and loving material beings present to the imagination, for we do not know any others. The same is true of all notions of this sort. God is truly a father, but the only fatherhood we can represent to ourselves is that of a living being begetting other living beings, and we know very well that God is not a father in the same sense as the man who begot us. *How* God is a father we do not know. In other words, the divine fatherhood cannot be represented to us. In a daring statement, whose only fault is that it can upset persons of strong imagination and weak mind, A.-D. Sertillanges, OP said with full justification that, from the perspective just described, the Thomist doctrine of our knowledge of God is "an agnosticism of representation."[2]

What is true of the notions of goodness, beauty and others of the same kind is in the first place true of the notion of *ens*. All the names given to God are names of creatures, even that of *ens*. We have no experience of something that is not created, composite, and even partly material. Now the notion of being accompanies all our representations, for to call something good, beautiful, true, or a father, is the same as saying a being that is good, beautiful, true, or a father. It is often said, and rightly so, that in the final

---

2. [A.-D. Sertillanges speaks of "an agnosticism of definition" in his *Le christianisme et les philosophies* (Paris: Aubier, 1939), pp. 268–273. See Gilson, *Le Thomisme: Introduction à la philosophie de saint Thomas d'Aquin,* 6th ed. (Paris: Vrin, 1965), p. 129 n83, 5th ed. trans. Laurence K. Shook as *The Christian Philosophy of St. Thomas Aquinas,* with a catalogue of St. Thomas' works by I.T. Eschmann (New York: Random House, 1956) p. 458 n37.]

analysis all our concepts are only the concept of a being variously modified. The simple fact that God is above a being, and that for the very same reason the proper meaning of the word, when it is said of God, cannot be represented to us, entails the consequence that none of the names we give to God, even if they are absolutely and positively true on the level of human knowledge, *represents* any perfection of God *such as it is in him.*

Hence the statements, which are surprising to some but literally true, in which the theologian asserts unequivocally that in our present state we know with certainty *that God is* but we do not know *what he is.* In fact, God is being itself and nothing else: *Deus est esse tantum,* but because for us being is always such and such a being, we cannot represent to ourselves a being whose whole nature would be being, neither more nor less. We should recall the concise, complete, and perfect statement on which we are centering our reflection: Our intellect can only grasp something that has a quiddity participating in being. Now the quiddity of God is being itself. Hence it is above our intellect: *sed Dei quidditas est ipsum esse, unde est supra intellectum.* Once again, St. Thomas avoids saying that God has no essence. As always, he identifies God's essence, and even his subsistence, with being: *est ipsum esse subsistens (EE* 4).[3] But in this unique case, since the essence is being itself, it surpasses understanding.

St. Thomas has often repeated this truth about God, which is the one most essential for the mind to grasp. *Esse* (being) has two meanings. In one sense it signifies the act of being (*uno modo significat actum essendi*); in another sense it signifies the composition of the proposition which the mind makes when uniting the predicate to the subject. Taking being (*esse*) in the first sense, we cannot know the *esse* of God any more than we can know his essence, but only in the second sense. We know in fact that the proposition formed about God when we say "God exists," is true, and we know this from his effects (*ST* 1.3.4 ad 2m): *Non possumus scire esse Dei, sicut nec essentiam.* It would be impossible to go further along this line; but we must go this far, and once convinced of this truth, we must not let it slip away from us, for the whole theology of human knowledge of God hangs on it. We know the

3. [ed. Roland-Gosselin, p. 34; trans. Maurer, pp. 55–56.]

proposition "God exists" is true and demonstrated as such, but we do not know what "exists" means in the proposition. If we do not know the meaning of *exists* in the proposition "God exists," we do not know what God is. Need we recall that the mind can form many true propositions about God? Nothing is more certain, but that is not the point at issue. St. Thomas affirms, repeats and holds absolutely that these propositions, though true of God, nevertheless do not make us know God's essence. They make us know what it is true to say about God as the cause of created perfections. Regarding God himself, whose essence is being, *esse* remains unknown to us in this life: *Esse Dei est ignotum* (QDP 7.2 ad 1m).[4]

This is a hard saying and many refuse to accept it, but everything depends on the level on which the soul in its quest for God inquires about the knowledge it can obtain of him. Scripture certainly speaks of God in terms designed to teach us about his nature, and thus by prayer, meditation and reverence to lead us to a real familiarity with him. The God He Who Is is identical with the God of Abraham, Isaac and Jacob, and not with that of the philosophers and scholars. Nevertheless he is the true God to whom the Christian speaks heart to heart as Father, Son, and Holy Spirit, especially as Jesus Christ, whom human eyes have had the happiness to see, and in whom we have the even greater happiness of believing without seeing him. It is unnecessary to look for any other. Those who show surprise that theologians with their speculations make the knowledge of the saving truth needlessly so complicated would be right if speculative theology, along with the philosophy it involves, were necessary for salva-

4. The bond uniting the thesis of the divine unknowability for us in this life to the identity of *essentia* with the divine *esse* is strongly underlined in the Disputed Question *De veritate* 2 ("De scientia Dei"). 11, resp. See the text of the Fourth Lateran Council, Decree 3, *Damnamus ergo,* etc ("The resemblance between the Creator and the creature is such that their still greater dissimilarity cannot fail to be observed"), cited in the *Motu proprio Doctoris Angelici* of Pope Pius X, 29 June 1914, [a translation of which is appended to] Jacques Maritain, *St. Thomas Aquinas,* trans. Joseph W. Evans and Peter O'Reilly (New York: Meridian Books, 1958), pp. 215–221 at 217.

tion. But that is not the case. The problems that occupy our mind at present only arise for those who, anxious to penetrate as far as possible into the understanding of faith, look for an abstract formulation of what natural reason can grasp and say about the meaning of the divine word. Theologians have given different replies to the question: What do we know, in the proper sense of the word "know," about the nature of God? All, however, have believed in the same saving God. All the pious familiarities are legitimate and good, but here it is a question of something else. Speaking strictly and as a philosopher, what *representation* can we form of God? The correct reply to the question is simple: If to represent God means to represent his essence, we cannot form any.

There is nothing in this conclusion that should disconcert a Christian or disturb his piety. Quite the contrary, for, first of all, as we have just said, everything any Christian believes, thinks or loves about God because of his faith and charity, the theologian also thinks and cherishes in his heart. We should be able to conceive God as St. Thomas Aquinas did and to love him as St. Francis of Assisi did. In the second place, Thomistic theology opens up perspectives on piety and mystical contemplation which are exclusively its own and which are of inestimable value; for the removal of the God of Christian faith beyond every conceivable representation avoids the deadly peril of anthropomorphism, which has turned away from God so many excellent minds to which, under the name of God, are offered finite objects that cannot be God and that are unacceptable to their reason. But this theology does even more. It offers for our love an unknown God whose infinite and inexpressible grandeur, defying knowledge, can only be embraced by love. The Christian religion admits of many different spiritualities; none is loftier than this one.

Thomistic theology has room for this particular spirituality only when it is taken integrally and strictly, without a sweetening that would weaken it. It cannot be said too often that St. Thomas never imposes anything of his own; he only prescribes the faith. As for the ways of understanding it which he proposes, we are committed to them only insofar as we assent to them. The elements of his doctrine that we do not understand remain true even if, because of our personal inadequacy, we cannot assent to them. What we ought to be able to avoid, in any case, is then to reduce the doctrine to the parts of it that we can understand. This all-too-frequent method of making a doctrine acceptable usually results in emasculating it and rendering it ineffectual, if not false. In any case, the doctrine then loses its identity.

We cannot overemphasize the harm done to truths by those who protect them against themselves by substituting half-truths for them. Like a doctor who is afraid to administer the full doses of medicines, the one who acts in this way does not kill his patient but he lets him die. If it is a matter of speculative truth about principles, it can only be completely hit upon or completely missed. We should not only assert, then, that the human mind is incapable of "understanding" God. This is too evident to be worth saying. Neither will we be content to say that in this life it is impossible to represent the divine being completely, perfectly or adequately. This is true, and we can stop there if we adopt a theology different from that of St. Thomas. But once his theological notion of God and his anthropology are granted, the only possible conclusion is the one he himself drew from them: *non possumus scire esse Dei*. We know that the proposition "God exists" is true; we also know the truth it signifies, for it affirms the simple, pure, and infinite *esse* of God himself. But we must also realize that it only signifies our human way of conceiving the divine being. It is true that God exists, and we know it, but in the case of God we do not know what the verb "exists" represents.[5]

5. This simply amounts to saying that, since our mode of knowing is what it is, we cannot know the divine essence in this life (*ST* 1.12.4). Now, there is no middle ground between seeing God's essence and knowing it such as it is in itself. On this point pagans and unbelievers are in the same position: "... ipsam naturam Dei, prout in se est, neque catholicus, neque paganus cognoscit" (*ST* 1.13.10 ad 5m). There remains, of course, the indirect knowledge of God through his creatures (*ST* 1.12.12), or, as St. Thomas himself says, "secundum aliquam rationem causalitatis, vel excellentiae, vel remotionis" (*ST* 1.13.10 ad 5m). Later, when we consider the Thomistic notion of participation in the order of existing, we shall see the metaphysical basis of this "analogical" knowledge of God. What we must keep in mind here is that a pagan and a Catholic can use the word "God" in the same sense, when one says "This idol is God" and the other replies "It is not God."

Such is the truth of the doctrine. Presenting it in all its rigor, St. Thomas has really only one reason for holding it, and that is because it is true. The oppositions it arouses in so many excellent minds, far from weakening it, confirm it, for the impossibility of representing to ourselves the being of God is due precisely to our properly human mode of knowing by means of quidditative concepts abstracted from sensible experience. If all quidditative concepts of an object are denied to us, it seems that the object itself is denied to us. Then the mind rebels and demands its rights.

The charge of agnosticism sometimes levelled against this part of Thomistic theology has no other source. St. Thomas was aware of the difficulty for he felt it himself. He was human like ourselves, and we cannot think without images, which is just what we are called to do in demanding that we affirm the being of God without in any way imagining what God is. But, precisely, every being that can be imagined is an act of being limited by an essence, whereas the pure being of Him Who Is is not limited by any determination. It is the infinite ocean of entity of which St. John Damascene spoke: *quoddam pelagus substantiae infinitum, quasi non determinatum.*[6] Accordingly, this being, completely undetermined by any essence, can in no way be imagined or represented by a mind whose natural and proper function is to define all its objects by their essences or quiddities.

This explains the natural, and therefore inevitable, embarrassment the human intellect feels when it is put in a position of affirming the existence of a being whose essence it cannot conceive. The progress of an abstraction that is deliberate, persistent and almost forced, because it is contrary to its present mode of knowing, leads the mind step by step to strip its object of everything it contains that is still capable of representation. He Who Is

---

They know enough about God (by his effects) to be able to agree or contradict each other in this matter. But neither of them knows the nature of God such as it is in itself, that is, *facie ad faciem.*

6. Aquinas, *Scriptum super Sententiis* 1.8.1.1 ad 4m, ed. Pierre Mandonnet and M.F. Moos, 4 vols. (Paris: Lethielleux, 1929–1947), 1: 196. [Cf. John Damascene, *De fide orthodoxa* 1.9, ed. E.M. Buytaert (St. Bonaventure, New York: Franciscan Institute, 1955), p. 49.17.]

is not a body, but because everything we imagine is a body, God is not imaginable; and because we cannot conceive without imagining, God is not properly speaking conceivable. And this is not all, for after having removed from God every material determination, we must also strip from his notion all the intelligible determinations found in creatures: matter and form, genus and difference, subject and accident, act and potency, with the result that, as this metaphysical abstraction progresses, God resembles less and less anything we might know. The final stroke is given when the mind is placed in the situation of conceiving a being whose only essence is itself, for this amounts to the mind's conceiving a being without an essence, which is something it is impossible for it to do. Hence the perplexity it feels at this thought: *et tunc remanet tantum in intellecto nostro quia est, et nihil amplius; unde est sicut in quadam confusione* (then there only remains in our intellect [the knowledge] that it is, and nothing more; and so it experiences a certain confusion).[7] Those who are disturbed by this impasse should realize that they share it with all humans and that St. Thomas himself suffered from it before them.

Why, then, expose oneself to it? Because the whole of theology is at stake. There is a time for representing God and a time for not knowing what he is. The latter is the most perfect knowledge of God accessible to us in this life. It is the theologian's greatest reward if, as is here the case, his theology includes in its structure the philosophy it uses and the mystical theology to which it is open at its summit, being all that at one and the same time without losing its unity: *velut quaedam impressio divinae scientiae, quae est una et simplex omnium* (like an imprint of the divine knowledge, which is one and simple, yet extends to everything: *ST* 1.1.3 ad 2m).

We understand these matters well only when we can express them in simple terms. Let us say, then, that, after having made the necessary attempts to ascribe to God the most perfect conceivable essence, the theologian must take upon himself another, immeasurably more difficult, process of refusing to represent God under the aspect of any of his creatures, no matter how lofty it may be. In short, after having tried to conceive God from creatures, he

---

7. *Scriptum super Sententiis* 1.8.1.1 ad 4m, ed. Mandonnet–Moos 1: 196.

must make an even greater effort not to conceive him as any one of them, though they are the only beings we can really conceive.

Nothing is more difficult to do, because, for us, to know is usually to become assimilated to what we know, whereas in this case we are asked to transcend all likeness. What do we know of something different from what we know, precisely as different? Yet this is exactly what we must affirm of God without being able to represent him. St. Thomas, with Dionysius, calls this "negative theology."[8] This does not take anything away from affirmative theology, for if we affirm nothing of God what would we have to deny in order to transcend it? On the contrary, it is a surpassing of what we know of God in order to locate him beyond everything we can say of him: a difficult effort because it goes against the bent of our nature. We cannot think of God without representing him as *a being*. The temptation recurs every time we think of him; and every time the theologian is beguiled by a concept exemplified by an image he should say "no" to it.

Perhaps the idea of doing this would not enter the mind of one who is only a philosopher. Why would a person want to go beyond what he knows and get involved in what he does not know? A philosopher always keeps watch in the heart of the Thomistic theologian, and this philosopher would also like to retain the illusion that he knows God's essence; but He Who Is has no other essence than being, and how can this pure *Is* be conceived? So we must have the courage to go beyond all representation and knowledge, to the extent that we do not know without images, in order to immerse ourselves in that ignorance of what God is and to reach him in the darkness beyond what we "know" of him. In the words of St. Augustine, we know God best by not knowing him: *melius scitur nesciendo* (*De ordine* 2.16.44).[9] St.

8. [St. Thomas speaks of the knowledge of God by negation and affirmation. See *Expositio in librum beati Dionysii 'De divinis nominibus'* 7.4, ed. Ceslai Pera (Turin: Marietti, 1950), §§729–732. See Dionysius the Pseudo-Areopagite, *De divinis nominibus* 7.3, ed. Regina Suchla, Corpus Dionysiacum 1, Patristische Texte und Studien 33 (Berlin and New York: Walter de Gruyter, 1990), pp. 197–198.]

9. [*De ordine* 2.16.44, ed. W.M. Green CCL 29: 131.16.]

Thomas says nothing different but gives the strongest reasons in support of it.

If we are to obtain the courage to enter into that darkness (*caligo*) where, precisely, God dwells, we must receive it from him by asking him to grant it to us. St. Thomas has expressed this so well that we cannot do better than let him speak:

> God is progressively better known to the extent that he is known as further removed from everything that appears in his effects. That is why Dionysius says in *The Divine Names* that he is known as the cause of all things, by placing him above them, and by denying them of him. For this advance in knowledge the human mind receives its greatest help when its natural light is strengthened by a new illumination, such as the light of faith, of the gift of wisdom, and of the gift of understanding, thanks to which, as has been said, the mind is raised above itself in contemplation, knowing that God is above everything it can naturally comprehend. But the mind cannot penetrate to a vision of God's essence. It is also said that the mind is, as it were, driven back upon itself by the brightness of that light. That is why Gregory, glossing the passage of Genesis (32:30), where Jacob says 'I have seen God face to face,' observes that 'When the eye of the soul turns to God it recoils at the flash of his immensity.'"[10]

Dionysius says the final word of the speculative theology of St. Thomas Aquinas: In the present life our best knowledge of God is a learned ignorance. There is nothing more positive than this negative method, which first gathers together all the true affirmative propositions we can form about God and then denies them of him because our mind cannot fathom the extent to which God transcends them. In fact, the perfection of pure being surpasses all of them infinitely.

---

10. Aquinas, *Expositio super librum Boethii de Trinitate* 1.2 resp., ed. Bruno Decker, Studien und Texte zur Geistesgeschichte des Mittelalters (Leiden: Brill, 1955), pp. 66–67 [cf. *Thomas Aquinas: Faith, Reason and Theology*, trans. Armand Maurer, Mediaeval Sources in Translation 32 (Toronto: Pontifical Institute of Mediaeval Studies, 1987), pp. 22–23].

5

Beyond Ontologies

... ipsum esse ejus videbimus, quod est ejus essentia
(*Summa theologiae* 1.12.6 ad 1m).[1]

As the saying goes, we should not dispute over words: *de nominibus non est curandum.* St. Thomas quotes the proverb with approval, for this is the attitude of the wise man. However, he was not
content with approving it: he put it into practice. It has been said
with good reason that he was surprisingly free in his language.[2]
Everyone who studies him closely experiences the fact, and this
can cause some trouble when the meaning of that freedom of
expression and its reason are not well understood.

When St. Thomas seems to use indiscriminately metaphysical
terminologies from different sources, to the scandal of the historian of philosophy, he acts as a good theologian, not as a neg-
ligent philosopher. By far, his preferred philosophical method is
that of Aristotle, the Philosopher, but he is aware that certain
other philosophers have come quite close to the truth and have
expressed it in different ways which, though undoubtedly less
correct, are nevertheless worthy of consideration. This is all the
more true because some of these philosophical languages were
taken over by highly authoritative theologians like Augustine,
Dionysius, Hilary of Poitiers, John Damascene, to mention only
the greatest Christians. Though St. Thomas wanted to acquire the
most rigorously precise language possible (and we can always
know which one he preferred), he never claimed to replace traditional theology with a new, completely personal doctrine. As a

---

1. [" ... we shall see his being itself, which is his essence."]

2. Ludger Oeing-Hanhoff, *Ens et unum convertuntur: Stellung und Gehalt
des Grundsatzes in der Philosophie des hl. Thomas von Aquin,* Beiträge zur
Geschichte der Philosophie und Theologie des Mittelalters, Texte und
Untersuchungen, Bd. 37, Heft 3 (Münster: Aschendorff, 1953), p. 3.

theologian, he teaches nothing else than *sacra doctrina*,[3] which is substantially identical with the deposit of faith and which has remained the same for everyone, at all times and in all places. What we can try to do is to advance a little further in understanding the faith and in so doing to bring to theology a more rigorous scientific precision, but it would be better not to attempt it if the price of this progress were a breaking with tradition.

So we must not be surprised to see St. Thomas avoid putting himself forward as he advanced in the understanding of revealed data and the teaching of the Church. His main concern is not that of a philosopher who is always quick to assert his difference from his predecessors. On the contrary, it is that of a theologian who, when he thinks he ought to use different language or employ old words in a new sense, is above all concerned to make sure that what he says is the very same as what his predecessors had already said.

Historians will never be reconciled to this attitude, which is the very negation of the literal truth of history, which is a little dull but respectable in itself. At this point we shall carefully avoid two opposite mistakes. The first is to want to justify historically interpretations that are historically unjustifiable. The historian can only ascribe to Augustine, Dionysius, and Boethius the ideas they themselves seem to have had in mind when writing their works. The attempt to say what these ideas were is difficult enough, and mistakes are often made; but, after all, if the historian does not do it, it is precisely what he sets out to do. There is no second-class truth; no matter how unimportant the matter may be, the adequation of the mind and reality always deserves the same respect.

The second mistake would be to want to reduce theological truth to that of the history of doctrines. We come back here to the tragedy of our times: the forgetting or the misunderstanding of the prerogatives of wisdom *par excellence*. History must be given its own domain, its methods and its rights. Relying on a philosopher's authentic statements, no historian would agree to ascribe to him ideas for which there is no reason to suppose they had been in his mind. In the history of ideas, what was unknown to a philosopher is of no interest to the historian. But theology is like

3. [For the notion of *sacra doctrina* see the Translator's Introduction, p. xvi with n25.]

an impression of the divine science, which, being one and simple, knows everything at once. The word of God contains in a higher way all the knowledge that in the course of time can be progressively gained through the effort of the theologians. In solidarity with this progress, the theologian is accordingly only one member of a spiritual family whose work he continues. As he makes his own contribution to it, he is not forgetful of those who went before him, but when he recalls their work it is rarely to criticize it as outmoded. Rather, it is to show that these theologians *had already tried to express* the truth that he himself now expresses, a little better perhaps, but identically the same truth.

Let us make an effort, then, to read the theology of St. Thomas as a theologian, and we should do this not as a lesser alternative, for as soon as the historian can rise to this perspective, which surpasses that of history, he will experience the same surprise as the philosopher who happens to take a disparaging view of past philosophies. It is very true that every doctrine, taken in itself, expresses nothing more than the thoughts of the philosopher himself, but he has not necessarily seen the whole truth of his own doctrine. Recall the important analogy proposed by St. Thomas at the beginning of the *Summa theologiae* (1.1.3 ad 2m): theology is related to the other sciences as the common sense is related to the five senses.[4] The *sensus communis* itself neither sees nor hears; that is the business of the external senses. But, being a superior power, it receives, relates, and judges the data of the five senses from a more general perspective. The theologian does something similar. Turning to the various philosophies and theologies, he first rejects with no false complacency what he perceives in them as out of place or, even worse, as false, but in some of them he discerns, as though hidden there, truths richer than those their authors were conscious of knowing. On the contrary, he himself arrives at a clearer perception of them because, coming after these authors and being in their debt, his natural reason

---

4. [For this analogy see Gilson, *Elements of Christian Philosophy* (Garden City, New York: Doubleday, 1960), pp. 32–33, 86–89, and *The Christian Philosophy of St. Thomas Aquinas*, with a catalogue of St. Thomas' works by I.T. Eschmann, trans. Laurence K. Shook (New York: Random House, 1956), pp. 204–205.]

went further along the same route, illuminated for him by the light of revelation.

The most striking instance of this sort of progress in theology is the notion of God. Christians have always known that he is Being, but they needed time to state more precisely the meaning of a term whose content in fact exceeds our grasp. According to Augustine, being means immutability,[5] and that is true. Being, he adds, is *essentia*, essence or entity, and that too is true. It can also be said that God is nature, for we speak of the divine nature; or that he is substance, since the Son is consubstantial with the Father. The liturgy itself approves this language: *in essentia unitas*.[6] This language is correct; and, what is more, we have no other, for it is the only one in which the Church has recognized the exact expression of its faith during a centuries-long inquiry approved by irrevocable dogmatic decisions. Moreover, here is the starting point of the theologian's attempt to gain an understanding of the saving truth. While engaged in this, he observes that, like the language of scripture itself, the one he is bound to use is a human language, designed to express the truth about things rather than about God. Then, without changing a word, but deepening and purifying its meaning, he fills it with the greatest amount of rational truth which – to the extent to which he himself understands it – this language can bear. God, then, is nature, but the divine nature is, if the expression is allowed, the *natura essendi*. God is likewise substance, but not in the sense of *sub-stans*, for he is not *under* anything. God is substance insofar as he is the very act of being in its absolute purity. Again, God is truly essence, because the *essentia* or entity of "that which is" constitutes for us the very reality of being. That is why the theologian, wanting to say that in the beatific vision the elect will know God such as he is and not a creature in place of him, however noble it may be, or a theophany, however brilliant we may imagine it, maintains that to see God "face to face" means "to see the divine essence." In this connection we should reread and

5. [Augustine, *Sermones* 7.7, ed. Cyril Lambot CCL 41: 75.158–159. See Gilson, *The Christian Philosophy of St. Augustine*, trans. Lawrence E. Lynch (New York: Random House, 1960), pp. 22–23.]

6. [In the solemn Preface of the Holy Trinity.]

reflect on the whole first question of the first part of the *Summa theologiae*, in which St. Thomas asks if a created intellect can see God *per essentiam*. We do not find him hesitating for a moment to use this word, for it is written of God (1 John 3:2): *Videbimus eum sicuti est*, and what would be a better rendering of "seeing God as he is" than seeing the essence of God? So the fact must be granted: *Unde simpliciter concedendum est quod beati Dei essentiam videant* (*ST* 1.12.1). Indeed, it will be granted *simpliciter*, that is, without qualification, for there is no qualification in the question that follows: What is the essence of God? To see God's essence is to see God such as he is. Now he is He Who Is, the infinite, pure act of being. On the one hand, then, when a created intellect sees God *per essentiam*, God's essence itself becomes the intelligible form of that intellect (*ST* 1.12.5); but at the same time, since the divine essence is identical with the pure act of being, to see God as he is consists in seeing that *esse* which is his essence: *videbimus eum ita esse sicuti est, quia ipsum esse ejus videbimus, quod est ejus essentia* (*ST* 1.12.6 ad 1m). At the same time, the object's proper mode of being determines the manner of seeing it "as it is."

Thus the theological language of St. Thomas is that of the universal Church, as his faith is that of the universal Church. But in offering the theology of St. Thomas to everyone as their guide and norm, the Church recommends, under the name of Christian philosophy, the special understanding of faith (*intellectus fidei*) which was the work of him whom it has chosen for its Common Doctor. At the center and as the heart of that teaching, which is in so many ways rich and varied, there is a certain notion of God, conceived as the unique being whose *esse* is his essence (*cujus esse est essentia*). The notion lends to that theology its properly Thomistic meaning. We must interpret in the light of *ipsum esse* everything St. Thomas says about God and even, as we shall see, everything his theology says about the beings that make up the universe; for what properly characterizes them is precisely the fact that, because they are beings, they are not *ipsum esse*.

Here once more the philosopher demurs. He would like to have everything the theologian says to him demonstrated, and as this philosopher is present in each one of us, it is not easy to satisfy him. Moreover, it is not a question of getting rid of him, but of doing justice to what is legitimate in his demand. Everything is not legitimate in it, for this philosopher too often seems to be ignorant of what theology is. Perhaps he does not even have a correct idea of metaphysics, for too frequently what he calls by this name is only a fiction of the imagination which he takes to be something evident to the mind.

Surprising as it might seem to those who have not tried it, it is very useful to approach the notion of metaphysics from theology, for the limits of metaphysics are more clearly seen, not at all by belittling it, for it is the highest human wisdom, precisely as human, but by comparing it with the Wisdom of God.

In opposition to critical idealism it is rightly claimed that metaphysics is a science; but, like every science, its demonstrations begin with principles which, just because it is from them that everything else in the science is demonstrated, are not themselves subject to demonstration. This is what St. Thomas says in his commentary on the *Metaphysics* 4.6.[7] After recalling the two primary conditions which the first principle should satisfy (that we cannot err in regard to it and that it is absolutely true), St. Thomas adds, "The third condition is that it is not acquired by demonstration or by other similar means, but that it presents itself almost naturally to the one who possesses it, as if it were naturally known and not acquired."

In fact, first principles are known by the light of the agent intellect and not at all by reasoning, but solely because the terms are understood. Summing up his doctrine, St. Thomas continues: "Thus it is clear that a very certain or very sure principle should be a notion such that we cannot be mistaken about it, that it be absolute, and that it be naturally known."

Such is indeed the first principle of demonstration, which is the principle of non-contradiction: It is impossible that the same thing be and not be in the same subject, at the same time, and in the same respect. This universal rule and primary condition of all coherent thought is absolutely and certainly true. Every human mind knows it spontaneously and naturally guides itself by it as by its very light. Nevertheless this rule of all knowledge does not itself produce any. The conclusions it ensures are worth no more than the notions about which it forbids us to think anything

---

7. [Aquinas, *Sententia super Metaphysicam* 4.6, ed. M.-R. Cathala and Raimondo M. Spiazzi (Turin: Marietti, 1950), §599.]

contradictory. This first principle of reasoning, then, presupposes a first principle of simple apprehensions. This principle is being, which is also very certain, absolute, and immediately conceived by the intellect in contact with sensible experience. What does the principle of contradiction teach us about it? That being is what it is and that it cannot be something else at the same time and in the same respect. But what is being? As Aristotle already said, this is the old question that is always in dispute and never completely answered.[8] Having established that the principle of contradiction is the first principle, metaphysics does not waste its time instructing us how to use it. This is the business of logic. The proper object of metaphysics is precisely to inquire what being is. In a sense, no one is ignorant of it, for nothing is thought except as a being, and as soon as anyone begins to think, he does so in conformity with this principle, which is the fundamental law of the mind. Its use is truly necessary, universal, and infallible. But who will claim that the answer to the question as to the nature of being is also evident? We cannot maintain that it is and at the same time denounce the errors of ontologism without precisely violating the principle of contradiction. For ontologism is nothing but a mistake about the nature of being. One of the first things we know with certitude is that being is, that it is what it is, and that it cannot be anything else, but to know what being is is a very different matter. It has been discussed for almost twenty-five centuries, and even Martin Heidegger has not yet discovered the answer.[9]

There is nothing very surprising about this; for if being is the first principle, there is nothing beyond it to which we can go in order explain it. To know it we must take our stand in it, within its concept; and since it is strictly speaking unlimited, transcending every particular object and including it, we can never be completely mistaken about it. What it is said to be may not be *being*, but unless it is nothing it *pertains to being*. The quest to conquer the first principle, so often described by St. Thomas,[10]

8. [Aristotle, *Metaphysics* 7.1, 1028b2–4.]

9. [For Gilson's views on Heidegger see *L'être et l'essence,* Problèmes et controverses, 2nd ed. (Paris: Vrin, 1962), pp. 365–377.]

10. [See especially *ST* 1.44.2 and *QDP* 3.5.]

from Thales and the "physicists" of Iona to those who at last have pressed on to the problem of existence, makes it clear enough that in this regard there has been genuine progress in metaphysics. Everyone should begin the attempt again for his own sake, and although it is easier now with so many guides, there are numerous enough occasions to fall into error. Some are still with Thales, but instead of saying "water" they say "energy." Others remain in the company of Anaxagoras, but instead of saying "intellect" they say "evolution." Still others, more courageous, press on to the viewpoint of Plato or Aristotle, from which being appears as the One or as Entity, substance or essence. The higher the mind rises toward the purely intelligible, the more the light dazzles it, the more it falters. It will be no surprise, then, that all the metaphysics of being do not exactly agree on what it is.

Once this is understood, we have still to realize that even when the metaphysics of being differ they do not, properly speaking, contradict each other. They do so only to the extent that, being incomplete, some of them deny the truth affirmed by those that have a fuller grasp of the nature of being. It could also be said that the metaphysics of this sort are true in what they affirm of being and false only in what they deny of it. This is also why, though each seems to be especially qualified to elucidate the particular realm of being it occupies, some of these metaphysics are truer than others because, while doing justice to those properties of being that others bring to light, they also know something else about it that they alone understand and that is perhaps the most important of all. The true metaphysics, within the limitations of human knowledge, is the one that, while affirming being as the first, most certain, absolute, and infallible principle, conceives it in such a way that through it and through it alone we can elucidate all the characteristics of beings given in experience, along with the existence and nature of their cause. If there really is such a notion of being, the metaphysics that claims it as its own is not simply truer than the others, it is true absolutely.

Which metaphysics enables us to see everything that the others see and more besides? In their quest for an understanding of faith theologians naturally turn toward the various metaphysics of being to use them for their own purposes. Did not God himself claim that his proper name is Being? Almost without exception, all Christian philosophies are philosophies of being. All throw light on one or more of its transcendental properties, and to that extent they are all true. It is good to know them in order to prefer the best. The beatific vision itself, though a totally face-to-face vision, admits of degrees. The separate Intelligences are arranged in orders and a hierarchy. Why would not the metaphysical understandings of being also admit of degrees of perfection? The search for the absolute truth must not come to a halt mid-way, but it is defensible at whatever point it may have reached. This comparison of wisdoms is worthwhile in itself and considerate of others, provided that it is conducted peacefully.

All the great Christian philosophies have something to teach us, and everyone is aware of the fact, for is there a single Thomist who, on the pretence of being more faithful to the Master, would refuse to read St. Augustine? The notion of a God whose essence is immutability because he is 'Is' opens the way to a dialectic of time and eternity whose object is man himself, the existent whom the stream of becoming carries along, consumed from within by his own lack of being and seeking to redeem it by an impassioned union with "I am and I do not change" (*Ego sum et non mutor*).[11] Augustine's cry is found in all the memoirs: *Quando solidabor in te?* ("When shall I be complete in you?")[12] It would be difficult to deny the truth of the ontology that inspires the *Confessions*. If this is not an authentic Christian philosophy and theology, there is none.

Duns Scotus raises another, more difficult problem, for he is not unaware of St. Thomas Aquinas. Coming after him, he does not feel that he can follow in his footsteps. What is that Thomistic *esse* that would be added to reality to make it exist, as though that which is had still to be made to exist? This is unintelligible to me, says Duns Scotus.[13] In fact, in his view being is the same as

11. [Augustine, *Contra Maximinum hereticum* 2.10, PL 42: 812.]

12. [These do not appear to be Augustine's actual words. Gilson seems to use them to express Augustine's longing throughout the *Confessions* and implicit in 11.30 (40), ed. Lucas Verheijen CCL 27: 215. See Gilson, *Philosophie et incarnation selon saint Augustin*, Conférences Albert-le-Grand 1947 (Montreal: Institut d'Études Médiévales, 1947), p. 47.]

13. [Duns Scotus, *Quaestiones in librum quartum sententiarum* (*Opus Oxoniense*) 11.3, in *Opera omnia* (Paris: Vivès, 1894), 17: 429 §46.]

essence, and since essence is being, it does not allow any addition: *nullum esse dicit aliquid additum essentiae*. Scotists are still of this opinion. And why oppose them? Essence is the object best adapted to the human mind in its present state. St. Thomas recognized the fact, as he recognized the difficulty of conceiving in itself that *esse* which, as the act of being of the essence, is itself not an essence. Why would the Scotist agree to substitute for a notion eminently satisfying to the mind one that even those who propose it claim it is difficult to conceive? There are difficulties no doubt, for reality, properly speaking, is not essence but the individual, and in the individual there is more than essence. Beginning with essence, how is individuality to be accounted for? The answer is well known, and the Scotist school often takes pride in its acute awareness of the individual. And rightly so; but haecceity occupies the place it does in Scotism only because it was necessary to work hard to find one for it. Scotism became a metaphysics of the individual because of the difficulty of explaining the individual starting with its own notion of being: a salutary warning for so many Thomists who confuse individuation and individuality. For, if the metaphysics of *esse* did not explain individuality better than the metaphysics of essence, there would be a point in considering it. But, as we know, *Unumquodque est per suum esse* (Everything is through its own being: *CG* 1.22.5). Though *esse* is not the principle of individuation, it is the first act of all individuality, and it is well to remember it.

But to repeat: what then is being? To this question Suárez and his disciples reply that it is real essence (*essentia realis*).[14] So they remain very close to Scotism. They specify, however, that real essence is not exactly the proper object of metaphysics. Rather, they would say, it is being insofar as it is being, in the complete indetermination of its notion, which prescinds from existence. Here the *reality* of the essence is not confused with its *actuality* or its *existence*. It is not opposed to the possible. Reality can be possible as well as actual. Thus understood, metaphysics has for

14. [Suárez, *DM* 2.4.5, Vivès ed. 25: 89. For Suárez's notion of real essence see Gilson, *Being and Some Philosophers*, 2nd ed. (Toronto: Pontifical Institute of Mediaeval Studies, 1952), p. 98.]

its object being in abstraction from existence. Metaphysical being is the same whether it exists or not.

This is the very opposite of Thomism. Yet, how often has Suárez been substituted for St. Thomas, ascribing to the latter a metaphysics in which being is divided into real and possible, opposing in it actual being to potential being, as though potentiality were anything else than a lesser actuality! It would be useless to argue, however, as those who tried it know well, for the Suarezians also have their reasons. They mistrust that *esse*, of which it is so difficult to form a distinct concept. It is as essences, and only as essences, these philosophers say, that created beings can become objects of science for our intellect.[15] What a strange science of created things, conceived such as they *would be* if they *did not exist*! But even that illusion has its usefulness. There are minds today which, in their enthusiasm for the Thomistic notion of *esse*, which they have just rediscovered, would be ready to sacrifice essences to it at the risk of making Thomism a forerunner of contemporary existentialism. But no being other than God would be possible without essences. Essence is the condition of the very possibility of the existence of finite beings. For us, essences – those images of the glory of the divine Ideas, those pure intelligible diamonds – must remain the reality itself of beings. But for this reason they must not be separated from existence, unrelated to which the possible itself is nothing.

The whole truth of Thomism becomes clear if we ask the following question: Is there a single characteristic of being, as other Christian philosophies understand it, of which Thomistic metaphysics does not give an account? If the answer is "no," we shall ask this second question: Is there another doctrine that gives as complete an account of all the properties of being insofar as it is being? If once again the answer is "no," we must conclude that the Christian metaphysics of St. Thomas Aquinas speaks the very truth about its object. For to say of being, certainly not all it is, but all that the human mind can know of it in this life, is indeed to achieve the adequation of mind and reality in which truth consists. We cannot go beyond that.

15. Pedro Descoqs, *Institutiones metaphysicæ generalis: Eléments d'ontologie*, première tome (Paris: Beauchesne, 1925), pp. 100–101.

6

The Fundamental Truth

Et sic fit ut ad ea quae sunt notissima rerum, noster intellectus se habeat ut oculus noctuae ad solem, ut II *Metaphysicorum* dicitur (*Summa contra Gentiles* 1.11.2).[1]

Few philosophers avoid the temptation of philosophizing without other presuppositions than thought itself. Fichte yielded to it without reservation in building his well-known immense structure. No Christian philosopher has gone that far, but some of them do not conceal their displeasure when they are urged to consider and, if possible, to see a primary truth which as such cannot be demonstrated. That is why, holding the composition of essence and existence in finite beings as the fundamental truth of Christian philosophy, they could not tolerate the idea of leaving it as an arbitrary assertion and have tried to demonstrate it.

In order to avoid any confusion, let us say at the outset that the distinction (or composition) of essence and being in finite beings is indeed demonstrable under certain conditions, but it is extremely important to understand their nature.

An excellent study of the *De ente et essentia* reduces to three the main types of arguments by which St. Thomas establishes the famous scholastic distinction.[2]

1. ["So it comes about, as is said in *Metaphysics* 2, that our intellect is related to the most knowable things as the eye of an owl is related to the sun." See Aristotle, *Metaphysics* 2.1, 993b9.]
2. [See the study of Aquinas's distinction between essence and existence in] M.-D. Roland-Gosselin, *Le 'De ente et essentia' de s. Thomas d'Aquin*, Bibliothèque thomiste 8 (1926; Paris: Vrin, 1948), pp. 187–189. This study, which has become a classic, sets forth "the arguments by which St. Thomas establishes the distinction between essence and being in creatures" (p. 187). Norbert del Prado undertakes something different in his *De veritate fundamentali philosophiae christianae* (Freiburg:

The first, which certainly originates in Avicenna but which St. Thomas could have read in the works of William of Auvergne, is clearly set forth in *De ente et essentia* 4: "Everything that does not belong to the concept of an essence or quiddity comes to it from without and forms a composition with that essence, for no essence can be conceived without its parts. Now, every essence or quiddity can be conceived without knowing anything whatsoever about its existence. I can conceive what a man or a phoenix is and yet not know if they exist in reality. It is clear, therefore, that being is other than essence or quiddity."[3]

The argument is irrefutable, but what does it prove? First of all that actual being is not contained in the notion of an essence. As Kant will later say, in the notion of a hundred thalers the notion of a thaler is the same whether it be a question of simply possible thalers or real thalers.[4] Next, as St. Thomas explicitly says, it proves *quod esse est aliud ab essentia vel quidditate* (that *esse* is other than essence or quiddity). For an essence to pass from possibility to being, then, an external cause must bestow actual existence on it. No Christian theologian or metaphysician has ever doubted the soundness of this conclusion. Because a finite being is not the cause of its own existence, it must hold it from a higher cause, who is God. In this sense, what is called the distinction between essence and being simply means that every finite being is a created being. Now all theologians grant this, but many refuse to conclude from it that a finite being is composed of two metaphysical principles: its essence and an act of being through which it exists. It is one thing to say that the essence of a finite

---

Consociatio Sancti Pauli, 1911). In the latter work it is a question not only of reporting the arguments of St. Thomas himself, but also of devising new proofs for the distinction (or composition) of essence and existence in finite being.

3. [*EE* 4, ed. Roland-Gosselin p. 34; trans. Maurer, p. 55. For William of Auvergne see my remarks in the introduction to *On Being and Essence*, pp. 23–24; see also Gilson, "La notion d'existence chez Guillaume d'Auvergne," *Archives d'histoire doctrinale et littéraire du moyen âge* 15 (1946): 55–91.]

4. [Kant, *Critique of Pure Reason* A 599/B 627, trans. Norman Kemp Smith, 2nd ed. (London: Macmillan, 1933), p. 505.]

being does not contain the cause of its being, which is all the dialectical argument of Avicenna, taken up by William of Auvergne and St. Thomas, proves. It is another thing to say that in this same finite being existence comes from an *actus essendi* to which it owes precisely its actual being. This by no means follows from the above argument.

Here is a good subject for meditation! Excellent philosophers and theologians have devoted their lives to the study and teaching of the Thomistic doctrine without ever suspecting the true meaning of this fundamental thesis. They have seen in it only a formula, a little more abstruse than others, for saying that every finite being is contingent and created. If nothing more than this were involved, every theologian without exception would teach the distinction between essence and existence, which we know well is not the case.

Let us move on to the second group of arguments. They are said to have the following general form: "There must be only one being in which essence and existence are not distinct, whose essence itself is its existence, because it could not be multiplied without being diversified, and there is no way in which it can be diversified. Hence being is distinct from essence in all created beings."[5]

Once again, the argument is conclusive, and now it results in establishing the truth of the distinction between essence and existence. Here is undoubtedly the theologians' royal and favorite road, for if God is the pure act of being he is the only one who can be it. What would lay claim to this title would be *ipsum purum esse*, and this would be God. That is why so many Thomistic theologians often accuse of pantheism those who, deaf to their arguments, deny the distinction between essence and existence in finite beings. These theologians give themselves an easy advantage, for in order that their demonstration be conclusive it would first be necessary to establish that, for God, to be Being is to be the pure act of *esse*, whose essence is being itself. Hence the value of the argument depends entirely on the validity of a certain

5. Roland-Gosselin, *Le 'De ente et essentia' de s. Thomas d'Aquin*, p. 188.

notion of God which, whatever its real worth, never seems to have entered the mind of many theologians, some of whom were saints.

The proofs in the third group, "drawn from the nature of created being, corroborate these conclusions."[6] The historian summarizes them for us with great subtlety. Since by definition it is caused by another, "created being does not subsist by itself, as the being whose essence is to exist subsists necessarily. On the other hand, being an effect cannot be a property of created being because of being itself; otherwise every being would by essence be an effect, and there would not be a first cause. Hence being an effect is a property of created being by reason of a subject distinct from its being."[7]

Nothing makes us see more clearly the fundamental difficulty all these demonstrations face. The proof that, because created being is not essential to being itself it can only belong to being by reason of a subject distinct from its being, presupposes the conclusion it was intended to demonstrate. For if we grant the premises of the argument, how do they lead to the conclusion that the subject of created being is *really* distinct from its being? Now it is precisely this and nothing else that is at stake. Every theologian will agree that by definition a created being is not identical with its existence. It is not, because, being created, it must receive existence in order to be. But, on the other hand, for a created essence to exist it suffices that God make it exist, which properly speaking is to create it. It might be true that God cannot create a finite being without conferring on it an act of *esse* really distinct

6. Ibid., p. 188.

7. On this point Roland-Gosselin, ibid., p. 188 n4 refers to *Scriptum super Sententiis* 1.8.4.2. See *CG* 1.22, 1.43, 2.52. He also refers to what he says of Avicenna's doctrine in his own work, on p. 152. But Avicenna's problematic is different from that of St. Thomas. It aims to prove that, if Being-through-itself is necessary, every other being is only possible, and consequently must possess its existence from a creative power. From this, Avicenna does not conclude that finite being is an essence in potency with regard to an *esse* distinct from it and which, because it is its act, makes it a being.

from its essence, but supposing this to be demonstrable, the argument has not demonstrated it.

These arguments, and all those of the same type, are alike in presupposing the conception of being, not in the sense of a being (*ens, habens esse*, that which is), but rather of the *act of being* (*esse*) which, combining with essence, makes of it precisely a being, a *habens esse*. Now, as soon as this properly Thomistic notion of *esse* is conceived, there is no further problem; there remains nothing more to demonstrate.

To be convinced of this we have only to refer to the texts of St. Thomas which his interpreter cites by way of proofs. Two things clearly stand out in them. First of all, that the notion of pure being (*ipsum purum esse*) thus understood is always presented in them as something taken for granted. Second, it is taken for granted in them only because, for the theologian, it is the proper name of God. To think pure *esse* is to think God.

The progressive dialectic of the *Summa contra Gentiles* leads St. Thomas to establish "that in God being and essence are the same" (*CG* 1.22). He already conceives, then, the possibility of their distinction. Now, if he does conceive it, the question is already answered. Indeed, engaged here in establishing God's simplicity, St. Thomas must deny of him every conceivable distinction. That is what he does in demonstrating, with Avicenna, that when there is a necessary being (*tertia via*) it exists of itself. Now it would not exist of itself if it had an essence distinct from its being, for in this case its being would belong to that essence and depend on it (*CG* 1.22.2). More briefly, and even as briefly as possible: "Everything is through its being. Hence, what is not its being is not through itself a necessary being. Now God is through himself a necessary being. Therefore God is his being" (*CG* 1.22.5).

It is impossible to go further along the same road, for only one other operation would remain to be carried out *if this were possible*. This would be to prove that the necessity of *necesse esse* is indeed the same as the necessity of what St. Thomas calls *ipsum esse*, the pure act of being, beyond essence itself, which in this unique case is as it were consumed by it. Now it must be admitted that a great number of theologians are in doubt about this notion or even dispute its validity. As far as we know, St. Thomas himself nowhere gives a demonstrative proof of it. No doubt he argues, "If the divine essence were other than its being (*esse*), the essence and being would thereby be related as potency to act. But we have shown that there is no potency in God but that he is pure act. God's essence, therefore, is not other than his being" (*CG* 1.22.7). This is undeniable, but the conclusion would be the same if, instead of conceiving being as the act of essence, it were simply conceived as the actual essence itself. Far from being unthinkable, such a notion of God seems to be common to all the theologians who, coming before or after St. Thomas, have adopted a metaphysics of being different from his own.

St. Augustine never thought of God in any other way than in terms of essence. Commenting on the 'I Am' of Exodus, he explains its meaning as follows: "In fact, since God is the supreme essence, that is, since he supremely *is*, and therefore is immutable, he has given being to the things he has created from nothing, but he has not given them the supreme being he himself is. He has given to some more being and to others less, and thus he has arranged natures according to the degrees of their essences."

There can be no misunderstanding this notion of God. Finite essences are arranged in a hierarchy according to the degrees of being. At the summit there is the supreme essence, which is not more or less but purely and simply the highest essence. Being the fullness of essence, it has nothing to gain or lose. The sign of its supremacy in the order of essence is its immutability. We should weigh St. Augustine's words themselves, as he tries to understand better (*perspicacius intelligere*) what God said to Moses through his angel in Exodus 3:14: *Cum enim Deus summa essentia sit, hoc est summe sit, et ideo immutabilis sit* ... .[8] St. Thomas is far from denying any of this. On the contrary, he finds in these words the starting point of the fourth way (of proving the existence of God), *ex gradibus quae in rebus inveniuntur* (from the degrees found in things [*ST* 1.2.3]). This is all very well, and the mind can stop there. He himself, however, takes a further step. Penetrating more deeply into this *summa essentia* which is called 'Is' (*Est*),[9] Thomas adds, *et haec Dei essentia est ipsum suum esse* (and this essence of

8. [*De civitate Dei* 12.2, ed. Bernard Dombart and Alphonse Kalb CCL 48: 357.7–11.]

9. [For *est* as the name of God see Augustine, *Sermones* 6.4, ed. Cyril Lambot CCL 41: 64.71–72; see also below n18.]

God is his very being [*CG* 1.22.7]). Thomas grants very correctly and without reservation that God is the supreme essence. He simply specifies that the sole essence God has is his being: *Deus igitur non habet essentiam quae non sit suum esse* (God, therefore, does not have an essence that is not his being: *CG* 1.22.2). This is the exact moment when we go beyond the theology of Augustine and enter that of Thomas Aquinas. The transition presupposes that we have already conceived, or that we conceive at the same time, the notion of being as an act beyond essence, or, if you prefer, that of an essence whose whole essentiality is being. Augustine had no idea of this; neither had John Damascene nor Anselm of Aosta. Alerted by Thomas Aquinas, John Duns Scotus preferred to stay on the path opened up by St. Augustine, adding to it, in the spirit of John Damascene, the important precision introduced by the notion of the divine infinity. *Ens infinitum*, for Duns Scotus, is the proper object of our theology. There is no room for uncertainty here, for he too, as was only natural, commented on the 'I Am' of Exodus, and in his interpretation he does not refer to the Thomistic *esse* but to the Augustinian *essentia*. Not only is God essence, but perhaps he is the only one who is. God is an *entitas realis, sive ex natura rei, et hoc in existentia actuali*. Or, in the language of Augustine himself, because being most truly and properly belongs to God, we should say that he is most truly essence: *verissime dicitur essentia*.[10]

So we come back to the same problem: In order to interpret the statement of Exodus, where, when, and how did St. Thomas demonstrate that, on the level of being, it was necessary to go beyond the notion of a being (*ens*), conceived until then as a simple notion, to divide it into two others, namely essence and being (*esse*), and then to assert that one of these two notions, namely being (*esse*), denotes *within a being itself* the supreme perfection and actuality of the other? St. Thomas clearly crossed this threshold. The only question is: how did he justify it? No reply is forthcoming. If he delivered the proof, neither Duns

10. See the texts in Gilson, *Jean Duns Scot: Introduction à ses positions fondamentales*, Études de philosophie médiévale 42 (Paris: Vrin, 1952), p. 227.

Scotus nor Suárez understood it or was convinced by it, and they were no mean metaphysicians.

The only reasoning that resembles a proof begins with the contingency of creatures. If essence is other than being in a finite being, being and essence must coincide in God in order to preserve his simplicity. But, as we have seen, the non-necessity of a finite being does not require that it actually be composed of essence and being. The point would be expressed no less exactly if we were to say, along with most theologians, that the actual existence of a finite substance, whose essence of itself is a pure possibility, is contingent. A finite being does not possess its existence from itself. In order to be it must receive being from necessary being, which is God. But this is in no sense a proof that in order to confer actual existence on a finite being God must concreate within it an essence endowed with an act of being which, though distinct from it, forms with it a being (*ens*) or that-which-has-being.

If it is difficult to find a proof of this, it is not because St. Thomas neglected to speak of it. When he does talk about it, however, it is usually to say that, without a limitation of the act of being by an essence, this act will be the pure act of being and it will be infinite, that is, it will be God (*CG* 1.43.5). Thus everything depends here on the Thomistic notion of God: "We have shown (*CG* 1.22) that God is his subsistent being. *Therefore nothing besides him can be its being.* So it is necessary that in every substance besides him the substance itself is other than its being" (*CG* 2.52.2). This amounts to saying that, if the essence of God is his being, everything else must be composed of being and an essence other than this being. And nothing is clearer *if* it has really been demonstrated that God is the pure act of being. Now, as we have seen, eminent theologians either have not read that truth in the text of scripture; or, even alerted to the fact that it was there, they have not been able to bring themselves to acknowledge it is there. They did not find it in scripture for the simple reason that it did not enter their mind.

Here we are apparently caught in a kind of dialectic, the two terms of which perpetually evoke each other. God is pure being because, if in him essence were distinct from being, he would be a finite being and would not be God. Conversely, the essence of a finite being is other than its being because if its *essentia* were identical with its *esse*, that being would be infinite and it would be God. There are external signs of this difficulty, of which it will suffice to mention one: the very widespread resistance the Thomist notion of *esse* meets not only, as is natural, in other theological schools, but even in the one claiming the name of St. Thomas Aquinas. And that is curious, to say the least, but it is a fact.

The worst attitude to adopt in the face of this difficulty is to deny its existence or to banish it from the mind as an annoying thought. The Church recommends Thomism as the norm of its theological teaching. How would it have made this choice if the doctrine in the last analysis were based on a vicious circle? The objection should not be made that here it is not a matter of philosophy but of theology. That is true, but it does not remove the problem. St. Thomas's theology is a scholastic theology. Its object is God, known through his word, but it tries to understand it, and it cannot do this without bringing into play the resources of philosophy. A master must have the skill to train the servants he employs for his service, and these servants must exist and be themselves in order to render the services he expects of them. If the theologian put into play a philosophy that would be nothing but a disguised theology, as long ago Averroes very unjustly accused Avicenna of doing, he would deceive himself before deceiving others.

There is no more frequent objection made to scholasticism. Authentic Lutheranism on the one hand, and philosophical rationalism on the other, have never ceased accusing it of corrupting everything: the word of God by philosophy, and philosophy by faith in a revelation unsupported by reason. The persistent attempts of certain Christian philosophers to clear themselves of the suspicion of teaching a "Christian philosophy" have no other source than the fear of seeing themselves charged with a hybrid speculation that is neither faith nor reason:[11] something equally contemptible to those who are

11. [Fernand Van Steenberghen accused Gilson of establishing "a kind of speculation intermediary between philosophy as such and theology": see his "La IIe journée d'études de la Société thomiste et la notion de 'philosophie chrétienne,'" *Revue néoscolastique de philosophie* 35 (1933): 539–554 at p. 545. Gilson replied that he never dreamed of

concerned to preserve intact the supernatural transcendence of faith, and to those whose absolute respect for reason resists every compromise with the irrational, or, what amounts to the same thing for them, anything superrational.

Here it is fitting to recall the bitter controversies that have made Christian speculative thought so unproductive, but we should not dwell on them.[12] First, because the controversy is quieting down. Though it was necessary at one time, it itself was an inferior form of mental exercise. Above all, however, because it is not in one's power, speaking for the truth, to dispose minds to receive it, and lacking this, his words are really addressed to the deaf. It is good, however, to speak to oneself, to open one's mind to the truth, and to oppose the accusation of giving way to prejudices, with the firm resolve not to entertain any of them, neither those with which we are charged, nor those with which they who impute them to us are unconsciously imbued. After all, it is not certain *a priori* that all the sins against reason are on the side of those who profess to be its true witnesses and claim to monopolize its use. Too many scholastics have forgotten the true nature of philosophical knowledge because they yielded to the unfounded demands of some of their opponents. It was they, however, and not their opponents, who stood for the full use of reason in its complete independence.

We cannot admire enough the attitude of these scholastic philosophers who are well aware of having two wisdoms at their disposal and find it so easy to divide their domains. "Wisdom, or perfect science," one of them said, "is twofold: one that proceeds by the supernatural light of faith and divine revelation, the other that proceeds by the light of human reason.

---

inventing this monster: see *Christianity and Philosophy*, trans. Ralph MacDonald (New York and London: Sheed & Ward, for the Institute of Mediaeval Studies, 1939), p. 95 and n16.]

12. [For the controversy in the 1930s over the validity of the notion of Christian philosophy see Bernard Baudoux, "Quaestio de Philosophia Christiana," *Antonianum* 11 (1936): 487–552; Maurice Nédoncelle, *Is There a Christian Philosophy?* trans. Illtyd Trethowan (New York: Hawthorn Books, 1960), pp. 85–99.]

The latter is philosophy, the former is Christian theology, a science supernatural in its roots and by reason of its principles. Philosophy, then, will be defined as knowledge of ultimate causes proceeding by the natural light of reason."[13]

These statements are completely true and they conform to the teaching of St. Thomas. They raise no problem as long as we remain on the level of formal distinction. Problems pile up, on the contrary, if it is claimed that these two wisdoms cannot live and work together in the same person, in the same mind. Will philosophy have nothing to say about the teachings of theology, a science whose principles are supernatural? And will theology give no thought to the teachings of philosophy, which proceeds by the light of natural reason? St. Thomas, at least, asserts the exact opposite, for he holds so strongly the formal distinction of the two lights and the two wisdoms only to allow them to collaborate better, without any possible confusion, but intimately and without any false scruples. St. Thomas wanted to make the natural light of reason penetrate right into the most secret parts of revealed truth, not in order to do away with faith and mystery, but to define their objects. Even the mystery of transubstantiation can be formulated in philosophical language. But the opposite relation can be established as well, for the theology of St. Thomas has the right of inspection in its philosophy, and it does not neglect to exercise it for the greatest good of philosophy. Those who claim the contrary are mistaken, and if they do it for apologetic reasons they miscalculate, for there is no other effective apologetic than the truth.

What is most remarkable in this regard is that they would like to separate revelation and reason to satisfy the requirements of a notion of philosophy that never existed. No philosopher ever philosophized about the empty form of an argument lacking all content. It is one and the same thing to think of nothing and not to think. If we mentally remove everything specifically religious in the great Greek philosophies from Plato to Plotinus, then everything specifically Christian in the philo-

13. Joseph Gredt, *Elementa philosophiae aristotelico-thomisticae* 1.1, 2 vols. (Freiburg im Breisgau: Herder, 1929–1932), 1: 1.

sophical speculation of Descartes, Malebranche, Leibniz, even Kant and some of his successors, the existence of these doctrines becomes incomprehensible. A religion is needed even to make it stay "within the limits of reason." The importance of Comte in this regard is that, having decreed that theology was dead and its transcendent God forgotten, he realized that in order to build up a philosophy whose tenets would be drawn from science, he had to look for the principles outside of science. In order to find them, he created a new religion and substituted for the God of Christianity a Great Fetish, furnished with its church, its clergy, and its pope.[14] The early "positivists" were indignant about this as a deviation from the doctrine, but Comte knew what positivism is better than they. They understood nothing about it, as can be clearly seen in the pitiful history of their "absolute positivism," reduced today to a verbal dialectic whose object is science, but for whom science itself becomes incomprehensible. For all wisdoms draw life from the highest among them, and if religion is eliminated, metaphysics dies with it, and philosophy in its turn dies along with metaphysics. Neoscholasticism is not immune to this malady; when it wanted to be a-Christian, it quickly degenerated into an abstract formalism whose utter boredom is bearable only by its authors, for to bore is not always boring. Sometimes it is asked with concern why this philosophy is so lifeless. The reason is that it is deliberately tied to a metaphysics that has no object.

There is a twofold mistake in saying that the object of metaphysics is the *concept* of being as being, explicitated in the light of the first principles. First, metaphysics does not treat of the concept of being as being any more than physics treats of the notion of becoming. If they did, these sciences would be turned into logics. Physics has to do with changing being itself, as metaphysics has to do with being insofar as it is being. We

14. [See Gilson's discussion of Comte in *Recent Philosophy: Hegel to the Present*, by Etienne Gilson, Thomas Langan, and Armand Maurer, A History of Philosophy, ed. Gilson (New York: Random House, 1966), pp. 275–276; see also Gilson, *Choir of Muses*, trans. Maisie Ward (New York: Sheed & Ward, 1953), pp. 103–130.]

emphasize, with being itself and not only with the concept of being. Nothing can be inferred from the concept of being as being; everything can be said about being as being. But for that we must first reach it, and if we do not comprehend it, at least we get in touch with it, and then never lose contact with it, under pain of losing our way in an empty verbalism.

The facility enjoyed by the dialectician is his greatest danger. It is always possible to begin with nominal definitions of being, substance, and cause in order to deduce their consequences with the help of the first principle. If it cannot be done easily, it can at least be done successfully. Some even do it with the mastery of virtuosos that compels admiration, but they gain from it nothing but an abstract sketch of a possible metaphysics. At best, they give themselves the pleasure of picturing it to themselves after the event, portrayed all at once in a kind of synthesis that enables them to embrace it with a single glance. But at that moment it is lifeless; they should not have gone about it like this in the first place. From this arises the deadly conflict between the mode of exposition and the mode of invention. For those who "exhibit" are very rarely those who invent; or when they are the same, while exhibiting they conceal from us their act of invention, so that we ourselves do not know how to reinvent by following in their footsteps, which is, however, the only way to learn. Then, too, when lectures are afflicted with this curse, we see students learning without understanding, while others lose confidence in their own philosophical abilities, even though the best proof of these abilities is that students at least realize that they do not understand.

These tendencies are particularly hard to explain in masters who claim to follow Aristotle's philosophy and defend its sound empiricism against the idealism of their contemporaries. Professing in all matters to begin with experience, it is paradoxical for them to turn away from it in metaphysics, whose principles govern the whole body of knowledge. Nevertheless, Aristotle's work is there, and if one is not interested in how it was constructed, the repeated statements of its author should be a sufficient warning of the danger.

Speaking of the absolutely primary rules of judgment, namely the principles of non-contradiction and the excluded middle, Aristotle points out that each scientist uses them as valid within the limits of his own science (*Post. Anal.* 2.11, 77a22–25). When it is a question of the knowledge of reality, one does not reason about reality *from* principles but *in agreement* with them and in their light.

It does no good to praise Aristotle's method if we refuse to follow it, and above all if we misconstrue its meaning. The last chapter of the *Posterior Analytics* is extremely important in this regard. Aristotle speaks there of the knowledge of principles. The assumption that they are innate is absurd, because if they were we would possess, *unknown to ourselves,* knowledges more certain than any demonstration. On the other hand, how could we formulate these principles within ourselves without having a faculty or power to acquire them?

What is this power? In order to satisfy the conditions of the problem, it is necessary, Aristotle says, "that that power be superior in accuracy to the knowledge itself of principles (*Post. Anal.* 2.19, 99b31–34). This statement has been interpreted to make it say less than it does, but in vain, for however the agent intellect is conceived in Aristotle's doctrine, even if it is reduced to the status of an indeterminate light and as indifferent to the intelligible apprehensions it causes, the statement of the *Posterior Analytics* means that this light belongs to a higher order and certitude than that of the principles it makes us know. It is not easy to state clearly St. Thomas's opinion on the subject, but we have to get used to a certain way of not understanding, which is nothing but a modest stance in the face of a purely intelligible object. One who understands everything is in great danger of understanding badly what he understands and not even to suspect the existence of what he does not understand.

The obscurity surrounding the origin of principles is exactly the same as that which partly hides their nature. It is agreed that in the Thomistic epistemology the agent intellect immediately conceives the principles by way of abstraction from sensible experience, and that is correct. It is added, then, that the intellect suffices for this operation, that it accomplishes it by its own natural light, without needing for its explanation to have recourse to the additional illumination of a separate Intelligence, not even, as some Augustinians would have it, to the light of God, the Sun of minds, the interior Master, finally the Word who enlightens everyone coming into the world.[15] And that too is correct, but it is not the whole truth. St. Thomas is the less scrupulous about not taking anything away from nature as, completely filled with the presence of God, like air with light, nature cannot be belittled without doing injury to the creator. Nothing can be denied to the essence of a being that God has made to be what it is.

In this spirit, at the very moment when St. Thomas in his *Summa theologiae* (1.84.5) places limits on the Platonic noetic of St. Augustine (*qui doctrinis Platonicorum imbutus fuerat*), he nevertheless holds the essence of the Augustinian thesis and the truth of his words. The intellectual soul knows material things in the eternal reasons, but this does not require the assistance of divine light added to that of the intellect. The latter suffices, "for the intellectual light within us is nothing else than a certain participated resemblance of the uncreated light, in which are contained all the eternal reasons (that is, Ideas). So it is said in Psalm 4:7, 'Many ask: who will make us see happiness?' The psalmist replies: 'The light of your countenance is imprinted on us, O Lord.' It is as though he said: Everything is shown to us by the very seal of the divine light within us." Thus, while maintaining the necessity of sensible experience at the origin of all human knowledge, St. Thomas intimately binds the human intellect to the divine light itself. It is because that light (which is the divine *esse*) includes, or rather *is*, the infinity of divine ideas (which are the divine *esse*) that the agent intellect of each one of us, being a participation in the divine light, has the capacity of forming intelligible concepts on contact with the sensible world. That intellect is not the divine light; if it were, it would be God. But it is a created product of that light, and in a finite way it expresses it and imitates its excellence. Hence its capacity to discover in beings, which are also made in the image of the divine ideas,

---

15. [John 1:9. See Bonaventure, *De scientia Christi* 4 concl., in *Opera omnia*, 10 vols. (Quaracchi: Ex typographia Collegi S. Bonaventurae, 1882–1902), 5: 22–24. See Gilson, *The Philosophy of St. Bonaventure*, trans. Illtyd Trethowan and F.J. Sheed (New York: Sheed & Ward, 1938), pp. 393–395.]

the intelligible forms in which they participate. The agent intellect in itself has the power to recognize outside itself the resemblance of the first cause, which is the source of all knowledge and intelligibility.

We shall have to return to this theme after trying to grasp St. Thomas's very special notion of participation. For the moment, let us simply examine that doctrine of knowledge such as it is; or, rather, let us attempt to do so, for how can we succeed? In one sense it begins by following Aristotle, but the genuine Aristotle who, from the level of sensation, sees empirical notions develop in an ascending induction, experience itself being the starting point of art in the order of becoming and of science in the order of being. But above science and its demonstrations there is an intuition of principles. Because demonstrations depend on principles, they themselves are not objects of demonstration. They do not provide science with its demonstrations; science does this for itself in their light. And since their light is thought itself, in the final analysis it is the intellect itself that is the cause of science (*Post. Anal.* 2.19). If this is so, why are we surprised that principles do not yield their full meaning always and to everyone? Their evidence and necessity themselves constrain the intellect which they rule by enlightening it, but which submits to them for want of being able to make their certitude that of a science, which the intellect itself would cause. The only way to approach these supreme intelligibles is with respect and modesty. The various simple formulas used to dispatch them in a few words are tautologies only for those who do not try to plumb their depths.

In a second sense – already implicit in the first and nourishing it from within and giving it infinite riches –, St. Thomas follows the Augustinian way, which itself belongs to Christian philosophy. What is astonishing is that, with St. Thomas, these two ways become one in his own doctrine. Even when he happens to name them, they can no longer be distinguished, for the two have become identical. The universe we know is henceforth composed of things created in the likeness of a God whose essence, that is to say, the act of being, is at once their origin and model. The intellect that knows these things is itself the product and image of the same God. In this doctrine, in which everything in nature is natural, but in which nature is essentially a divine product and a divine image, it can be said that nature itself is sacred. It is not surprising that the first intelligible object an intellect of this sort discerns in such a real world is the primary notion of being, and that with this origin this notion surpasses in every way the mind that conceives it.

Here is the truth dimly perceived by those who mistakenly teach the unity of the agent intellect. They are wrong in that respect, but it is true to say that Aristotle calls our agent intellect a light that our soul receives from God. In this sense it is even truer to say with Augustine that God illumines the soul, of which it is the "intelligible sun." These philosophical disputes over details lose their sharp edge from the theological heights we have reached. In Augustine's view, knowing is contemplating in the soul a reflection of the Ideas; in Aristotle's opinion, knowing is an act of the agent intellect throwing light on the intelligibility of the sensible world. The doctrines differ in structure, but in the final analysis they are in agreement: "It matters little whether we say that it is the intelligibles themselves in which the (intellect) participates from God, or that the light producing the intelligibles is participated."[16] In either case God is at the origin of knowledge.

From St. Thomas himself to his most recent interpreters this truth has often been lost from sight. Turned to folly, it was sometimes corrupted in ontologism. Reduced, in reaction, to the limitations of an almost physical empiricism, it cut itself off from its source, which is the being of God himself. Preserved in its fullness, it offers itself as a naturalism similar to that of the Greeks, but in which, owing to its dependence on God in its very being, nature is filled with a divine energy and so to speak always points to infinitely more than what it is.

Since this is true of knowledge as well as of being, it should be enough to banish the phantom of a metaphysics based on nothing but regulative formulas. Wisdom begins with notions that are certainly abstract but endowed with a content extracted from the real world by a mind whose light discovers in forms the light itself of which our mind is an image. For metaphysics, the primary notion of being is given to us before all others; it is at the same

16. Aquinas, *Tractatus de spiritualibus creaturis* 10 ad 8m, ed. Leo W. Keeler (Rome: Gregorianum, 1946), p. 133.

time apprehended as such and illuminated by the light of Him Who Is, the cause of every intellect and of every intelligible object. This datum, and the intellectual experience we take from it, is the true principle of metaphysics. All philosophical wisdom is virtually contained in the meaning of the word "is." So we should not make it a "starting point," as some call it. We must dwell on it at length and leave it only to come back to it as quickly as possible. Being is the most universal and evident of all notions, but it is also the most mysterious, as befits the very name of God.

This is the only reason for the differences among metaphysics. As Suárez very aptly said, it is evident *an ens sit* (that being is), but not *quid sit ens* (what being is).[17] *Ens* does not signify a word but a thing, and that thing is so simple that it cannot be defined but only described. Every metaphysics presupposes a notion of being, presented for the metaphysician's reflection, as a truth of that simple intuition which Aristotle justifies by the surpassing excellence of the intellect over the principles themselves that it posits. There is no science of the cause of science. Moreover, the controversies among great metaphysicians are fruitless as long as they oppose each other on the level of conclusions, without first confronting each other on the level of principles. But they do not like to compare their interpretations of principles, for they have the same first principle; they only understand it differently. No demonstration will make them understand it in the same way, as we see from the fact that all the great Christian philosophies continue to exist side by side. In all of them God is being. As Augustine says, "He is 'Is.'"[18] But for one, 'Is' means the Immutable Being; for another, that whose nature it is to exist (*natura existendi, natura essendi*); for still others being is real essence, the inner principle and ground of all the actions and operations of a subject. The objection should not be raised that these are concepts of real being, not of the being of reason which is the concern of metaphysics. If metaphysics were only directed to an abstract notion it would be nothing but a logic. As a science of reality, the first philosophy has for its object existing being, and

17. [*DM* 2 proem, Vivès ed. 25: 64.]
18. ["(Deus) non aliquo modo est, sed est est": *Confessions* 13.31 (46), ed. Lucas Verheijen CCL 27: 269–270.]

that is why, again in the apt words of Suárez (*DM* 2.2.29), if there were neither God nor angels there would be no metaphysics.[19] Everything happens as though the metaphysicians were dispersed within the same intelligible space, which is too immense for them to have the good fortune to meet each other.

There is no trace of skepticism here. We only ask not to be placed in the position of playing the role of the *indisciplinatus* by demonstrating that whose nature does not allow it to be demonstrated. Moreover, it can be demonstrated that the first principle is being. Even those who dispute it, as Descartes did in a certain sense, are obliged to use it.[20] What did he assert when he said "I am"? Finally, it is possible and even necessary for a metaphysician to relate at length the meaning he ascribes to the first principle to the contents of experience. If he can find a meaning of the word that does justice to all the properties of beings inasmuch as they are beings, and that arranges them in thought in the order they have in reality, the philosopher will give his assent to that notion without qualification, hesitation, or doubt. It will be his first principle, and most certainly, because as he conceives it this notion dispenses with all the others, for it includes them eminently, whereas all the others taken together do not measure up to its intelligibility.

Accordingly, metaphysics is a science from the moment when, having laid hold of the principle, it begins to deduce its consequences; but the fate of the doctrine depends on the understanding of the principle. A true metaphysician will rarely be caught in the act of contradicting himself. At the start he must adopt his doctrinal positions, and he must meditate at length on the mind's first approach to its formation of principles before committing himself to them. The capacity of the principle to elucidate reality under all its aspects will undoubtedly confirm its truth in the course of constructing the doctrine, but it is the principle's own

19. [*DM* 2.2, Vivès ed. 25: 79 §29. In §30 Suárez says that if no immaterial beings existed there would probably still be room for one part of metaphysics concerning being and the transcendentals.]

20. [See Gilson, *Being and Some Philosophers,* 2nd ed. (Toronto: Pontifical Institute of Mediaeval Studies, 1952), p. 109 for Descartes's attitude to existence or being.]

evidence, which the mind sees in the very act of conceiving it, on which its certitude essentially rests. Once the meaning of the principle is grasped, the doctrine unfolds in its light. It does not make the doctrine true, it simply makes its truth evident.

In teaching metaphysics, then, the main concern should not be the sequence of conclusions. Dialectic masters this so easily that it can correctly deduce all the conclusions of a principle without seeing its truth or understanding its meaning. This is the source of the impression opponents in a dispute have of always being misunderstood. And indeed they are, for each judges the other's sequence of conclusions in the light of his own understanding of the meaning of the principles.

This is not how the good teacher of philosophy proceeds. After lengthy reflection, he says what he sees and tries to lead others to see it. For this purpose, before undertaking to demonstrate what is demonstrable, he elucidates the truth that is indemonstrable to show the evidence for it.

This is a whole art in itself. As old as metaphysics, the art is so well known since Plato that there is no need to insist on it here. Starting with images, we must transcend them in order to reach, as by flashes of light, the intelligible principle. Though we only catch a glimpse of it, we can expect that this insight will arouse others to see it as well, as we proceed to an explanatory analysis of the contents of the notion. That will only happen by stepping down a little below it, every time we use our judgment to clarify its pure intelligibility. We can withdraw from it, provided that we do not for a moment lose our hold on it, as we must step back a little from a beautiful face in order to see it. The elucidation, then, should take place at the center of this intelligible insight itself. It need not be very extensive; it is sufficient for itself. As far as others are concerned, it can only lead the way to invite them to set out in pursuit. Moreover, because it is linked to the simple apprehension from which the first judgment springs, it will soon run short of words, as is all too evident from what has just been said about it.

7

The Keystone

... ea quae in diversis scientiis philosophicis tractantur, potest sacra doctrina, *una existens,* considerare sub una ratione, inquantum scilicet sunt divinitus revelabilia (*Summa theologiae* 1.1.3 ad 2m).[1]

Thoughts die when no one thinks them any more; then they no longer exist except in God. In the same way we can even let ways of thinking die, with their formal objects, principles, and methods. It is true that some are outmoded, but fewer by far than is believed; for there is scarcely a great monument of human thought which, however neglected it may be for centuries but revisited, fails to surprise us with what it still has to offer for our admiration and instruction.

The paradox of the present situation of Thomism in the Church is that, far from being forgotten or neglected by it, it is recommended to us and even prescribed as the norm of its teaching, but that many Christians prefer other theologies. It is not the business of theology or philosophy to reflect on this fact; only the Church's magisterium is competent to address the matter. It is better not to rake up these thoughts. Even the Thomist would prefer that what he freely assents to were not something as it were imposed from so high a level on others who, in their own judgment, cannot imagine anyone finding happiness in adhering with heart and soul to what they do not know, understand badly, or completely misconstrue.

Excuses can be found for them, the main one being the rarity and difficulty of theological knowledge. There is a great deal of it

1. ["... the one single sacred doctrine can treat objects that are the subject matters of the different philosophical sciences under one aspect, that is, insofar as they can be included in revelation."]

in books, but as long as it has not been brought to life again in the mind of a living person, he does not know what it is. To undertake to give it being, movement, and life goes beyond the capacity of most people, whose highest ambition in this regard must be limited to something far less than this. There are some philosophers who stand out in history. Similarly there are some theologians whose works we have; but we, the majority of readers, can scarcely do more than share in what is a true philosophical or theological thought *veri nominis*. Each of us takes from them what we can. Most of the time we think at second-hand.

The theologian himself knows this difficulty when, in his effort to put his thoughts into clear formulas – which is thinking properly speaking – he speaks to himself and to others. Instead of resting in the slow inner oscillation of a mind that sees conclusions in principles and vice versa, he must then descend from the stability of understanding to resort to the movement of reasoning. This is another matter. The obscure mass of knowledge flows down in slender threads, one at a time, not to say drop by drop. The pen does not write books, but phrases, words, letters, and finally marks, whose downstrokes and upstrokes enable thought to express itself only by elements separated in space and following each other in time. The last article of the *Summa theologiae* that St Thomas wrote is organically and vitally connected with the first, but the continuity linking them in the mind of their author exists in ours only by way of imitation, when it docilely reproduces a sequence presented to it from outside.

For these and many other reasons whose analysis would stretch to infinity, St. Thomas's theology as it is in itself does not easily come through to us. The most difficult obstacle to overcome, if we are to embrace it in itself and in its entirety, is the tendency so common today to divide it into two parts: a philosophy whose metaphysics would be for St. Thomas the counterpart of Aristotle's natural theology, and a "sacred doctrine" or supernatural theology based on revelation. Now it is very true that St. Thomas made a strict distinction between the two orders of the natural and supernatural, of reason and revelation, of metaphysics and theology properly so-called. Every attack on this distinction betrays his thought and his work. But it is also true that his own contribution to scholastic theology was precisely to give it a structural unity based, on the one hand, on his very special use of philosophy, by opening it to the light of revelation, which enabled reason to read new truths in it, and, on the other hand, his obtaining for revealed theology from philosophy, thus enhanced, a language, method, techniques, and notions whose use was valid enough, at least with the validity of analogy, to allow it to take the form of a science.

The main point is to see the truth of all these matters from a perspective that is at once universal in scope and yet simple, somewhat like the way God knows everything in the unity of his knowledge, which is his being. When we think of God's knowledge, we are not surprised that theology, which is but its limited and hazy approximate image, appeared to St. Thomas as no more than straw.[2] But there is no straw without grain. Worthless in comparison with God's knowledge, this theology is divine in relation to our own. Hence the restrained but passionate joy with which St. Thomas speaks of it. Doubtless this also accounts for his penchant for the summary "inductions" to which the saint often has recourse when the occasion arises. These panoramic views, in which the whole of reality, or at least an aspect of the universe, is completely unveiled to our sight in the organic unity of its structure and order, are perhaps the least imperfect human analogue of this integral, and integrally unified knowledge, which is the divine essence, that is, the divine being itself.

These stopping points along the road are the fruit of the theologian's analytical endeavor, whose methodology requires the division and subdivision of questions and replies, foreseeing objections and stopping to discuss them, brushing aside equivocations, but also running the risk of causing others by his desire to do justice to the truth in other doctrines or what is justified in other languages. Like a light that expands and scatters, the light of the mind decreases in intensity as it explicates itself.

2. [At Thomas's canonization process, Bartholomew of Capua testified that when St. Thomas was urged to complete his *Summa*, he replied: "I cannot, for everything I have written seems like straw to me, in comparison with what I have seen and has been revealed to me" (*Fontes vitae S. Thomae Aquinatis*, ed. D. Prümmer, M.H. Laurent [Toulouse: Privat, 1912–1928; Paris: Revue thomiste, 1928?–1937], p. 377).]

We must, then, take advantage of the rare occasions when the theologian gives himself up to the joys of theological contemplation, when his gaze embraces the maximum of truth in the simplest of insights. In the light of the intellect, reason easily traverses the infinite space between the first cause and the humblest of its effects. The fundamental distinction between what belongs to nature and what belongs to grace is certainly not forgotten, nor even less, obliterated, but if we look at things from God's point of view, it should allow us to grasp everything in a single glance, in the unity of an order in which all differences find their places.

Every attentive reader of St. Thomas knows moments like these and could cite passages in which the voice of theology itself is heard in all its purity. Here is one, rendered as faithfully as possible, when the thought of St. Thomas must be translated into a language less exact than his own, but faithful to his intention and respecting the perfect continuity essential to it. The original, which alone is authentic, speaks with an incomparable force. But to be exact, the purpose of this experiment is not to substitute a copy for an original. Quite the contrary; we should like to guide readers, students, and friends to him for their own good.

The question at issue is the following: "Does God have the power to beget?" (QDP 2.1). Fifteen arguments are given to prove that he does not, and, to tell the truth, it is easy to find some. The whole of Arianism is already firmly in place, occupying the ground for centuries, always driven back or contained, but coessential to natural reason itself. It can be granted that God is Being, but who could agree that he is a Father? That is possible only through faith in the Son. At the outset, then, it is certain that the question rightfully belongs to that "revealed datum" which by its very essence transcends the perspective of natural reason and thus constitutes the specific matter of theological speculation. No metaphysics will ever prove that God has the power to give birth. If he has, however, that truth will not be defined with the desirable accuracy without putting it in its place among others whose meaning natural reason can understand better without completely "comprehending" them. But let St. Thomas speak for himself in his own way and theologize as he pleases:

In reply, we must say that it is the nature of every act to communicate itself as much as possible. Thus every agent acts inasmuch as it is in act. Acting, moreover, is nothing else than communicating that whereby the agent is in act, as far as that is possible. Now the divine nature is the supreme and most pure act. Hence it communicates itself as far as possible. It communicates itself to creatures only by likeness, which everyone can see, for every creature is a being (*ens*) because it resembles that nature. But the Catholic faith ascribes to it still another way of communicating itself, insofar as that same nature communicates itself by a kind of natural communication, so that, just as the one to whom human nature is communicated is a human being, so also one to whom the divinity is communicated is not only like God but truly is God.

But we should observe in this connection that the divine nature differs from material forms in two respects. First, because material forms are not subsistent, so that human nature in human beings is not identical with the human being who subsists, whereas, on the contrary, the deity is identical with God, and consequently the divine nature is subsistent. The second difference is that no created form or nature is its own being (*suum esse*), whereas God's very being is his nature and quiddity, so that the name proper to him is *He Who Is*, as is clear from Exodus 3:14, for thereby he is given his name as from his proper form.

In beings here below, on the contrary, their form is not self-subsistent. So there must be something else in the subject to which it is communicated by which the form or nature receives subsistence. This is matter, in which material forms and natures subsist.[3] But since the material nature or form is not its being, it receives being, because it is received in something other than itself. It follows from this that it must have a diversity of beings according as it is received into a diversity of subjects. Thus human nature in Socrates and Plato is not one with respect to being, although it is one in respect to its essential notion.

3. "... materia, quae subsistit formis materialibus ...," literally: which subsists under corporeal forms, in the sense of the low-Latin *subsistere*: to support.

On the other hand, since the divine nature is self-subsistent, in the communication in which the divine nature is communicated there is no need of anything material in order that it receive subsistence. As a consequence it is not received in anything by way of matter, the result of which is that subjects thus begotten are composed of matter and form. Besides, because the [divine] essence itself is its being, it does not receive being through the subjects in which it would be. In virtue of one and the same being, then, that nature is in the one who communicates it and in the one to whom it is communicated. Thus it remains numerically the same in both.

We have a very good example of this communication in the activity of the intellect. The divine nature, being spiritual, is revealed more perfectly by spiritual examples. When our intellect conceives the quiddity of anything that is self-subsistent and outside the mind, there is a sort of communication of this thing which exists in itself. In fact, our intellect in a sense receives from the external thing the latter's form, so that when it exists in our intellect this intelligible form proceeds in a way from the external thing. However, since the external thing differs in nature from that of the knowing subject, the being of the form contained in the intellect is different from that of the self-subsistent thing.

All this remains true in the case of our intellect's conceiving its own quiddity. On the one hand, it is then the form itself understood by the knower that in a way proceeds into the intellect when the latter conceives it. A certain unity is then established between the conceived form which comes forth and the thing from which it comes forth. Indeed, both have an intelligible being, since one has the being of the intellect and the other that of the intelligible form, which is called the mental word. Nevertheless, since our intellect by its essence does not have a power of knowing that is perfectly in act, nor is the human intellect identical with human nature, it follows that, although the above-mentioned word is in the intellect and is in a certain way conformed to it, this word is not identical with the very essence of the intellect, but it is its expressed likeness. Moreover, in the conception of an intelligible form of this sort there is no communication of human nature, as there would have to be for one to be able to speak of a begetting in the proper sense of the term, which implies the communication of a nature.

Nevertheless, just as when our intellect understands itself it contains a word proceeding from it and bearing the likeness of that from which it proceeds, so also in God there is a Word bearing the likeness of him from whom it proceeds. This procession excels in two respects the procession of our word. First, as we have already said, our word is different from the essence of our intellect, whereas the divine intellect, being by its very essence in perfect actuality as a knower, cannot receive any intelligible form different from its essence. Consequently its Word is essentially one with it. Second, since the divine nature is its own actuality, the communication that takes place in it in an intelligible way also takes place in it in a natural way, so that it can be called a begetting. In this respect the Word of God excels the issuing forth of our word. This is the way Augustine describes this manner of begetting.[4]

But we speak of divine things in our own manner, which our intellect takes from things here below, from which it draws its knowledge. And because we never posit an action in the lower world without affirming a principle of the action, which we call a power, we do the same when it is a question of God, though in him power and action are not distinct as they are in creatures. And that is why, given that there is in God a begetting, which is a term signifying an action, we must grant that he has the power to beget and assign to him a generative power [QDP 2.1].

St. Thomas's method is clear. The theologian holds on faith that there is a Father and a Son in the Christian Trinity, but the relation of fatherhood and sonship that is well known to us from experience implies the power of begetting in the Father. The question, then, is whether we ought to speak of a power of begetting in God as in the finite objects of our experience.

If the answer is "no," what would happen? We would have to give up speaking of God the Father and consequently of speaking of Jesus Christ as the Son of God, our Savior. So the most immediate object of the Christian faith would be eliminated as

4. [Augustine, *De trinitate* 9.4–12, ed. W.J. Mountain and Fr. Glorie CCL 50: 297–310.]

meaningless. Instead of helping us to understand the Faith, theology would render it inconceivable to us.

Shall we say that God is truly a father but that he does not have the power to beget? The result would be the same, for indeed *de divinis loquimur secundum modum nostrum* (we speak of divine things in our own way); and this is our only choice, unless we simply give up speaking about them. Now everything we know that is able to beget has by definition the power to do it. To speak of a begetter without the power to beget is meaningless to us. Consequently, St. Thomas demands that the theologian take full responsibility for his language and that, having of necessity to use human words, he does not empty them of all conceivable meaning. God the Son is begotten by the Father, consequently the Father has the power to beget: *est potentia generativa in divinis* (in God there is the power to beget).

This is the affirmative phase of theology. But the theologian would not reach his goal if he let us believe that God is a father and that he has the power to beget in the sense in which that is true of the finite beings of our experience. Hence the understanding of faith, to the extent that it is possible, is going to require the theologian to try to go beyond these images and to eliminate from the notion of begetting everything that links it to finite being and would thus make it inapplicable to God.

This is what St. Thomas has just done, not only as regards the notion of begetting but also by an astute, critical interpretation of each of the examples he borrowed, as he went along, from the cognitive functions in which the intellect "conceives," that is, "begets," its concepts.

It is impossible to observe how he conducts this theological purification without noticing the principle from which it proceeds: the notion of God as the pure act of being, whose essence is identical with his being: *ipsum purum esse*, or *natura essendi*. There is no stage of this dialectic in which it is forgotten. On the contrary, this notion is so to speak its well-spring, sinews, and life: *ipsum esse Dei est ejus natura et quidditas; ipsa essentia est suum esse* (the very being of God is his nature and quiddity; the essence itself is his being). In us, on the other hand, *aliud est esse formae intellectus comprehensae, et rei per se subsistentis* (the being of the form contained in the intellect is different from the self-subsistent thing). At each step we find one of the procedures whose sequence is described in the two *Summae*: the reduction of action to power, of power to nature, of nature to essence, and essence to *esse*, that is, in the final analysis, to the 'Is' of Him Who Is.

Consequently it is IMPOSSIBLE to profess the theology of St. Thomas without at the same time subscribing to his notion of God, and by implication to his notion of being. Some think they are sufficiently in agreement with his thought by linking his theological conclusions to the notion of God conceived as Being; but this is not enough, if, at the same time, they do not conceive being as St. Thomas does.

This is the source of most of the difficulties some theologies run up against. They agree with St. Thomas in identifying God with being, but they are not truly in agreement because the being they have in mind is first of all that of essence (*essentia*, entity), or better, that of a being (*ens*) whose essence is simply placed in the state of existence by its cause. This being of essence is then presented to the mind as a primary idea, most often conceived as that of a simply possible being, indeterminate, unlimited, infinite, and universally predicable of everything that exists. This notion of being is like an abstract, formal counterpart of real being-in-general. But being-in-general does not exist insofar as it is general. Clearly, a notion like this cannot be directly obtained from experience. To explain its origin, then, there is an irresistible temptation to see our abstract idea of being as the form itself of our intellect, impressed on it by God, and in which everything in us is intelligible, as everything subsists in God in virtue of being his effect and created image. Hence, contrary to the real intention and explicit idea of these authors, they are blamed for teaching an "ontologism" of which they are innocent and which, moreover, they reject as strongly as possible.[5] But appearances are against

5. [Gilson likely has in mind Antonio Rosmini and Vincenzo Gioberti. Ontologism, which taught that direct and immediate knowledge of God is natural to us, was condemned in 1861; see Heinrich Denzinger, *Enchiridion symbolorum definitionum et declarationum de rebus fidei et morum,* 32nd ed. (Barcelona, Freiburg, and Rome: Herder, 1963), §§ 2841–2847. See Gilson's comments in *Recent Philosophy: Hegel to the Present,* by Etienne Gilson, Thomas Langan, and Armand Maurer, A History of Philosophy, ed. Gilson (New York: Random House, 1966), pp. 238–265.]

them; and we have seen famous masters in Thomistic theology needlessly lay themselves open to the criticism, which sometimes warrants a condemnation, for want of having discerned the true Thomistic notion of being or for having lost sight of it.

If we are to understand St. Thomas's doctrine, we must see that his noetic is completely dependent on a metaphysics of being, and that this metaphysics demands a notion of being such that it contains within itself, and presents at first glance, the link binding finite being to its first cause and what distinguishes it from that cause. From this initial moment on, it becomes equally impossible to conceive finite being as independent of its cause and to confuse it with that cause. Nothing exists without God, and nothing is God.

All theologians teach this; they differ only in the way they teach it. But these differences are important, if not directly for salvation itself, which is the specific purpose of revelation, at least for the understanding of the Faith, which is the specific purpose of theology. Now, on this point St. Thomas precisely affirms that the first notion the intellect forms *is not* a notion of being so indeterminate that it would be applicable alike to God and creatures. On the contrary, the first notion, which is the first principle in the order of simple apprehension, is that of a being (*ens*), befitting a creature conceived as "that which has being" (*habens esse*), and consequently inapplicable to God under this form. For God is not a being; he *does not have* being, he Is.[6]

6. This is what Christian philosophers have failed to see who identify in succession the *light of reason,* the *being* present to thought, the *essence* of being, and the *idea* of being. They equate them in order to facilitate the synthesis of a metaphysics of being of the Thomistic sort and a noetic of illumination of the Augustinian sort. But this is not the best way to go about it. The Augustinian interiority of God to thought is easily found in Thomism in the form of a general interiority of God to his creation. He is present to everything according to the nature of its being: to the soul as soul, to love as love, and to the intellect as intellect. In this sense, Being causes in us, as in a being endowed with intellectual knowledge, the abstract notion of being. The neo-Augustinians are unsatisfied with the mutilated Thomisms offered to them, and they are not wrong. But they would have spared them-

If we bear this in mind, we shall see why, because of this very truth, St. Thomas's proofs of the existence of God by way of causality are both possible and necessary. They are possible because, starting with a being, we can mount upward to being as the cause of what the being (*ens*) possesses of being (*esse*). They are necessary precisely because they do not begin with an indeterminate notion of being-in-general, but with the sensible experience of the being of some existing thing. So we could not discover in the notion of *habens esse*, by way of analysis and as it were *a priori*, that totally different notion of pure, self-subsistent *esse*, as though it were its own essence. So an inductive proof is necessary, whose only conceivable means is causality.

At the same time, we see the profound reason why the doctrine of St. Thomas, having been thus saved from ontologism from the very start, is immediately directed to that negative and transcendent theology that makes its own the most precious element in the heritage of Greek theology. For if we start with what has being, or "a being," affirmed as the proper object of the human mind, it goes without saying that pure being, which is God, naturally escapes our grasp. We cannot imagine a self-subsistent "Is" without the support of a "that which." Whatever name we might give to God, we must always add that in his case this name signifies his nature, which is his substance, which is his essence, which is *ipsum purum esse*. No representation of this pure being is possible. And that is why, in the last analysis, in this life we can only embrace God by love, beyond affirmations and negations, in darkness. Moreover, St. Thomas does not simply say that we know the being of God poorly; the word we have heard him use is "unknown." Remember his statement: *Esse Dei est ignotum* (The being of God is unknown).[7]

The absolute transcendence of God can only be properly expressed in a metaphysical language in which, speaking with the greatest possible precision, we can say that even *ens* is not exactly

---

selves the attempts to create a synthesis that was bound to fail, if they raised their reflection beyond the *idea* of being as it reveals the *essence* of being, to the act of being itself. Without the act of being, no theology can take the place of St. Augustine's.

7. [See *QDP* 7.2 ad 1m, cited above, p. 38.]

appropriate to God, for he is purely and exclusively that by which a finite thing is a being (*ens*), thanks to its participation in being (*esse*). No freedom of language could be allowed in this theology, for unless you follow it to the summit of this barren peak you miss its very notion. The conception of He Who Is gives us the only vantage point from which our knowledge of God, however slight it may be, offers at least a real analogy with that which God has of himself. God knows everything by knowing himself, and his self-knowledge is his essence, which in him is pure being. Theology, being one (science), is able to embrace in a single glance the whole of being, because it organizes itself around a notion of God similar to the knowledge he has of himself and of all things, around the very fact that he 'Is.'

We have just seen how things stand in discussing the notion of divine begetting. When St. Thomas begins to take up this essentially theological problem (whose solution, whatever it may be, must remain shrouded in mystery for us), he recalls in several lines rich in doctrine the purely metaphysical notion of the act of being, the most sublime among those with which we can honor God: *natura cujuslibet actus est quod seipsum communicet quantum possibile est ... . Natura autem divina maxime et purissime actus est* (it is the nature of every act to communicate itself as much as possible ... . Now the divine nature is the supreme and most pure act). So the divine nature will communicate itself to the fullest possible extent, and this can be done in two ways. First, as is clear to everyone, as a cause producing effects that resemble it. Second, as the Catholic faith teaches, by a sort of natural communication in which God begets a God. What is this? Metaphysics? Or a strange blending of reason and faith, of natural knowledge and revealed truth? Can we explain at one and the same time the possibility of the creation of the world and that of the begetting of the Word? Are we confusing philosophy and theology? No, and St. Thomas himself has indicated the point where he moves from one order to the other: *Sed fides catholica etiam alium modum communicationis ipsius ponit* (But the Catholic faith ascribes to [the divine nature] still another way in which it communicates itself). However, he does not confuse but unites, welcoming every truth, natural or supernatural, whatever its source may be, putting it in its proper place in thought corresponding to its order of dependence in being. Between God and his creation there is discontinuity of being, but also a continuity in the intelligible order, and reason can discover this continuity, provided that it begin with the true principle. On this condition, without compromising its unity, theology can include all things, considering them from the perspective of God's own knowledge of them. Then, even what we naturally know becomes revealable; for God knows everything, and there is nothing he knows that he would not be able to reveal.[8]

8. [For the notion of "the divinely revealable" see above n1, as well as the Translator's Introduction, pp. xv–xvi with n24.]

8

Causality and Participation

... creare convenit Deo secundum suum esse, quod est ejus essentia (*Summa theologiae* 1.45.6).[1]

All Christian theologians teach that the universe is the work of God, who created it from nothing by the free exercise of his power. It goes without saying that St. Thomas teaches the same doctrine, but he does not present it in the same way as the others, for if he affirms along with them that the proper effect of the creative act is to cause the being of creatures, his personal metaphysics of being affects the traditional data of the problem in two ways, concerning the notions of the creator himself, the act of creation, and the exact nature of its effect.

In God himself to whom does the act of creating belong? As we can foresee, the correct answer is that whatever in God is common to the whole divinity is the cause of all that exists. Nevertheless some theologians hesitate, for in the perspective of Christian theology the creation of the universe is not the first manifestation of the divine fecundity. In the words of St. Thomas himself, "the procession of the divine person is prior to, and more perfect than, the procession of creatures" (*ST* 1.45.6 obj 1). Indeed, the divine person comes forth as the perfect likeness of his source, but the creature only as an imperfect likeness. It seems then that the processions of the divine persons are the "cause" of the procession of things, and thus the act of creating properly belongs to the person.

St. Thomas does not deny this; quite the contrary. But we must see in what sense it is true. The Trinity as a whole is engaged in the work of creation, as is clear in the very words of

1. ["... to create belongs to God by reason of his being, which is his essence."]

the Church in the *Nicene Creed*. The Christian believes in the Father almighty, "creator of all things seen and unseen." Furthermore, he acknowledges that all things were made through the Son, and finally that the Holy Spirit is the Lord and giver of life. So the act of creating does indeed properly belong to the persons. Nevertheless, if we carefully consider the matter, the persons operate here as including God's essential attributes, that is, the attributes of the divine essence, which are intellect and will. A workman operates through the inner word his mind conceives and through the love his will has for the object of his activity. Similarly in God, the Father produces the creature by his word, which is the Son, and by his love, which is the Holy Spirit: *ex voluntate Patris cooperante Spiritu Sancto* (from the will of the Father with the cooperation of the Holy Spirit).[2] In other words, the divine persons here direct us back to the divine essence; they are indeed creative insofar as they include two essential attributes.

What do we mean by going back to the divine essence? God's essence is being itself. Now, to create is properly speaking to cause or produce the being of things: *causare, sive producere esse rerum*. Let us understand this correctly, and if necessary once again recall that basic notion of *esse* or being, conceived as distinct from that of *ens* or a being; for to the Thomist it is being, thus understood, that is here in question. In fact, "Since every cause produces something similar to itself, the principle of an action can be known by its effect. Fire is produced by fire. The act of creating (that is, the production of being) consequently belongs to God in virtue of his being, which is his essence (*creare convenit Deo secundum suum esse, quod est ejus essentia*), and because essence is common to the three persons, creation is not exclusive to one person but is common to the whole Trinity" (*ST* 1.45.6).

This notion is so to speak the very center of the theology of creation. As regularly happens every time it is a question of the notion of being, the mind hesitates between conceiving the cause from the effect, according to the philosophical order, or the effect in function of its cause, according to the theological order. The Christian philosopher does both, for he theologizes, and the theologian is not restrained from philosophizing. We can say, then,

2. [From the liturgy of the *Missale Romanum*.]

that since God is "being," (*esse*), and every cause produces an effect similar to itself, the proper effect of God is the being of the creature. To create is indeed *producere esse rerum* (to produce the being of things); or, conversely, since creatures are beings because they have being (*esse*), we can say, ascending from them to God, that in order to be their cause he himself must be the pure act of being: *ipsum purum esse*. As soon as we have grasped the Thomistic meaning of the notion of *esse*, the two ways are nothing but the two directions of one and the same way. As Heraclitus said, the road upward and the road downward are one and the same. We shall come back to this problem. For the moment let us be satisfied to deepen the notion of creation beginning with the notion of being.

Since the mind naturally proceeds to judge causes by their effects, our first statement will be that to create a being is to produce it from nothing: *ex nihilo*. In Thomistic theology that statement is often replaced with others, such as: *the emanation of total and universal being*, or *the emanation of total being from non-being or nothing*. These two statements are in agreement, but they do not bear precisely on the same aspect of the truth. The emanation of universal being often draws attention to the fact that, unlike the element of truth in philosophies such as those of Plato and Aristotle, there is nothing included in the notion of a being in general that does not owe being to the creative act. St. Thomas is thinking especially of matter, which no Greek philosopher thought of as created. On the contrary, in Christian philosophy, since matter exists it has being; so it is also an effect of God's creative omnipotence.

The first way leads to the second. Certainly the creative act causes everything in a being, in every sense of the verb "to be." But in its first and profound sense this verb signifies the act itself whereby a being is in some way posited outside nothingness. It is precisely this act of a being, its *esse*, that is the proper effect of the creative act. To produce a being (*ens*) in its very being (*esse*) is to produce it from nothing. Anything conceivable prior to creation must be something, some kind of being. But by definition every being possesses being, and since to create is to create being, that something prior to creation would itself be created. In the most profound sense, creation is the production of the total being (*totius esse*), because the creative act bears primarily on the *esse* of the *ens*, that is, on that which in everything included in the definition of the being makes it something that is. In a finite being there is nothing prior to that except what is not. But what is not is not even a *that which*. It is nothing; it is the negation of being. Hence St. Thomas's statement: the emanation of the total being, which is called creation, takes place *ex non ente, quod est nihil* (from nonbeing, which is nothing: *ST* 1.45.1).

If such is the nature of the creative act, it can belong to God alone. The effect of every other act productive of being is to cause a special way of being: being human, a tree, in motion, and so on. But creation produces being absolutely, which is the most general of all effects, since every other effect is only a particular way of being. Now the most universal effect can have only the most universal cause, which is God. St. Thomas often expresses this in a statement whose forcefulness is concealed by its simplicity: being is the *proper* effect of God. And indeed, since the proper name of God is He Who Is, and every cause produces an effect similar to itself, created being must resemble God first and foremost because it also is a being. Hence St. Thomas's oft-repeated statement that being is God's first effect because it is presupposed to all other effects: *Illud ... quod est proprius effectus Dei creantis, est illud quod praesupponitur omnibus aliis, scilicet esse absolute* (The proper effect of God the creator is that which is presupposed to all other effects, namely being taken absolutely: *ST* 1.45.5). But being cannot be said to be the proper effect of God without by the same token saying that God alone has the power to cause being or to create. The conclusion necessarily follows, for the first effect is the consequent of the first cause, and the first effect is being: *Primus autem effectus est ipsum esse, quod omnibus aliis effectibus praesupponitur, et ipsum non praesupponit aliquem alium effectum* (The first effect is being, which is presupposed to all other effects, and it itself does not presuppose any other effect: *QDP* 3.4). So the giving of being as such must be the effect of the first cause alone acting through its own power: *secundum propriam virtutem,* and by this we mean, not, as in the case of *all* other causes, inasmuch as it would have its efficacy from another cause (ibid.). Because it is creative, the first cause is the cause of all causality.

By way of parenthesis we would point out the futility of controversies that claim to refute conclusions beginning with principles other than those from which they follow. The Thomist proposition: "God alone causes being," has become a battleground among theologians of various schools, sometimes even among "Thomists." This did not happen up to the time of the excellent Bañez, who does not seem to have been troubled by it.[3] How, they ask, can a cause produce an effect without producing the being of that effect? They are right, but everything depends on the metaphysical level on which the question is raised. St. Thomas is very far from denying that beings are able to produce other beings. Quite the contrary, no one has more forcefully asserted the proper efficacy of secondary causes, but he has no less strictly refused to grant to these causes the power to produce the very being (*esse*) of their effects. All causes other than God are instrumental causes, whose being (*esse*) is received from the first cause, and whose causal efficacy is exercised on subjects whose being (*esse*) is similarly provided for them by the first cause. In other words, the causality of causes presupposes their being, which is caused by God alone, just as their effects, in order to be produced, presuppose that their matter, form, and all the elements included in their ontological structure, have been created and conserved by God. In strict Thomistic language (to which, however, St. Thomas does not always restrict himself), it could be said that the secondary cause causes everything in a being (*ens*) except its being (*esse*). Or again, and this seems to be St. Thomas's preferred formula, the secondary cause does not cause being, but being-such-and-such or being-this-or-that. He could not compromise in this matter, for to produce being *non inquantum est hoc, vel tale*, would be to produce being absolutely, and this would no longer be causing but creating.

Let us return now to the effect of the creative cause. This, we have said, is the very being of its effect. Here we encounter another notion which is very simple though often enough mis-

3. [According to Bañez, God alone produces being (*esse*); secondary causes can produce beings but without their acts of being: see Domingo Bañez, *Scholastica commentaria in primam partem 'Summae theologiae' s. Thomae Aquinatis* 1.3.4, ed. Luis Urbano, Biblioteca de Tomistas españoles 8 (Madrid and Valencia: Editorial F.E.D.A., 1934), pp. 154–158. See also Gilson, *Elements of Christian Philosophy* (Garden City, New York: Doubleday, 1960), pp. 175–176.]

understood – the notion of "participation." To participate and to
be caused are one and the same thing. To say that created being
is participated being is to say that it is the proper effect of the
uncaused being, who is God. That is why St. Thomas so frequently moves, without articulating the movement, from the ideas
of being-in-itself and the pure act of being to those of the cause
of all being, of being caused, and of being by participation. Here
St. Thomas is truly "at home," at the center of his metaphysical
and theological citadel. It is in this tangle of primary notions that
we discover the meaning of the principle continually advanced by
him, that "that which is by another is reducible, as to its cause, to
that which is by itself." At the same time we see that the notion
of being-by-another, or by a cause, is identical with that of being
per modum participationis. Finally, we see clearly the bond uniting
the notion of created or participated being to the Thomistic notion
of God, the pure act of being. "For we must posit a being (*ens*)
which is its very being (*ipsum suum esse*). The proof of this is that
there must be a first being which is pure act and in which there
is no composition. This unique being, then, must cause all other
beings to exist, which are not their being but possess being by
participation." Those who ask if St. Thomas thought that creation
is a notion accessible to natural reason alone will find the answer
to their question here. And this, our theologian says, is the
argument of Avicenna (*Metaph.* 8.7 and 9.4).[4] He then concludes:
"Thus it is proved by reason and held on faith that everything is
created by God" (*QDP* 3.5). And this agreement [between reason
and faith] is theological.

We must be on our guard here against conceiving participation as the act of "taking a part" (*partem capere*). St. Thomas does
not object to any language that is not absolutely unjustifiable, and
so he will also allow this "etymology." But the relation of the
participated to the participating in his metaphysics should be
understood as an ontological relation of cause to effect. If we
remembered this we would have fewer difficulties in interpreting
certain proofs of the existence of God, for example, the *quarta via.*
For, understood in their Thomistic sense, the relations of "by
another" to "by itself," which it brings into play, are relations of

4. [See above p. 21 with n3.]

effects to their efficient cause or they are reducible to them. This is true even of participation in the order of formal causality, by way of resemblance, for the form itself is nothing if it does not first have being. At the source of everything there is being-by-itself, which is the cause, and beings-by-another, which are its effects. Accordingly it is one and the same thing for them to be beings, to be the effects of the first cause, and to be participations of being-by-itself. We must try to examine these notions from all angles, to see them give rise to each other, and then to embrace them in a single glance, as one single truth.

The statements bringing to mind this group of notions can be easily recognized. For example: Everything that is such by partici-pation depends on what is such universally and essentially (often cited is the well known metaphysical hypothesis: *Unde si esset unus calor per se existens, oporteret ipsum esse causam omnium cali-dorum, quae per modum participationis calorem habent* (Therefore, if there were one self-subsistent heat, it would necessarily be the cause of all hot things, which have heat by way of participation: QDP 3,5). Or again: Being by participation comes after being by essence. And especially: What is such by participation is *caused* by what is such by essence. All these propositions often occur together, so that the proof that every being is created by God ends up as a proof of the existence of God, in which all the prior metaphysical intuitions – true but imperfect – of the best meta-physicians find their perfection in the light of the Christian notion of the pure Act of Being. St. Thomas knows very well that neither Plato nor Aristotle taught the concept of creation from nothing. Being a theologian, however, and regarding everything from a viewpoint analogous to that of God (*ut sic sacra doctrina sit velut quaedam impressio divinae scientiae*: so that sacred doctrine bears as it were the imprint of the divine knowledge [*ST* 1.1.3 ad 2m]), his insight pierces the clouds that still obscured their own truth from them. We must see him at work, boldly advancing beyond Greek metaphysics, which his own thought surveys with a single unin-terrupted movement. Here it is not a question of the history of philosophies such as the philosophers conceived them, but of a sort of collective journey to the truth, under the guidance of a theologian who himself follows the light of scripture, *velut stella rectrix*. Let us listen to him:

We must say that everything that exists in any way is from God. For if we find anything participating in anything whatsoever, it must be caused in it by that to which it belongs by essence, as iron is made red-hot by fire. Now we have shown above (q3, a4), when treating of the divine simplicity, that God is self-subsistent being itself. Furthermore, we have shown (q11, a4) that there can be only one subsistent being, just as, if there were subsistent whiteness it could only be one, since whitenesses are multiplied by the subjects that receive them. So all beings other than God are not their own being but participate in being. It is necessary, therefore, that all things that are diversified by their different ways of participating in being, which makes them be more or less perfectly, are caused by one first Being, which exists most perfectly. Thus Plato said that before all plurality there must be unity, and Aristotle says in his *Metaphysics* (2.1, 993b23–27) that what is supremely being and supremely true is the cause of every being and every truth, just as what is most hot is the cause of heat in everything else (*ST* 1.44.1).

Thus, after more than forty questions [in the *Summa theologiae*], one of the five "ways" to God,[5] which are so often reduced to their bare dialectical outlines, is unexpectedly presented as a philosophy of being, a theology of *esse*, a metaphysics of creation, participation, and causality. Nothing could give us a better idea of the theologian's perspective, from which truths are given as contained one within another, like their objects themselves, whose being is only conceivable by Being.

This is because discursive reason can only explore the wealth of the first principle by successive and separate probes. A dialectical process is needed to clear the entrances to it, then passageways, finally by deliberate reflections to provide those unifying insights whereby that which reason had to distinguish is reunited in the intellect's simple glance. Then we no longer have the simple anticipation we had at the start of a wealth to be itemized; neither do we have the open display of the many goods it conceals. Rather, we should speak of reconstituting by a mental

---

5. [That is, the fourth way.]

process the unity of being, as though sight could reunite the spectrum of colors in white light without losing them from view.

The person who makes an effort to reflect on the principles from within will avoid entering into futile controversies about the number and order of the ways to God, the question whether each is a proof distinct from the others, finally the problem of the exact moment in the development of the *Summa* when the demonstration of God's existence is really completed. There are as many ways to go to God as there are modes of being, and the development of any one of these ways could go on to infinity, like metaphysics itself. Being is inexhaustible.

Since we have no other possible method, let us retrace the thread of our reflections. [Q]*uodcumque ens creatum participat, ut ita dixerim, naturam essendi*: every created being participates so to speak in the nature of being (*ST* 1.45.5 ad 1m). What is this *natura essendi* but God?[6] We have then a created universe with a nature entirely its own, since every special being, by the very fact that it is being, participates in the nature of the divine being, not as a part participates in a whole but as an effect participates in its efficient cause. Created, then conserved by an action of the same nature as that which created it, a secondary being subsists at each moment of its duration only by the divine efficacy. If we are imbued with this notion, we face a new series of consequences that lead us to the heart of the Thomistic universe in its most literally sacred character.

It becomes clear that God is directly, essentially, and intimately present to the being of each of his creatures.

Since the first effect of God is the very being of things, the divine efficacy extends to creatures directly and immediately: First, because creation is God's own special mode of causality, and therefore in this case nothing comes between the cause and its effect. Second, because there is nothing the creature itself can receive without first receiving being. All the particular properties of being presuppose it. It is certain, then, that by his efficacy God is immediately present to each of the effects he produces.

6. [Gilson here adds a reference to St. Anselm's *Monologium* 3, in *Opera omnia*, ed. Francis S. Schmitt, 6 vols. (Seckau: Abbatial; Edinburgh: Thomas Nelson, 1938–1961), 1: 15–16.]

Now God's efficacy, power, and will are the divine essence itself. Where God's efficacy is present, there also is his essence: *ubicumque est virtus divina, est divina essentia* (QDP 3.7). So it is literally true to say that God is present to beings by his very essence. Moreover, it should have been possible to infer this conclusion directly from the fact that in the Blessed Trinity creation properly is the work of the divine essence, which is the divine *esse* itself. Thus the following propositions follow in sequence: God is his being; since every efficient cause produces its like, the proper act of Being is to cause being; caused being subsists only by the continuance of the creative action; created being is a participation in creative Being; finally, creative Being is present by its very essence to the created being that subsists only through it.

The above series of propositions clarifies the unique role played in this theology by the notion of being (*esse*), whose archetype and model, if we can use these terms, is God himself, as he revealed his name in Exodus. We should often recall this central point in the doctrine. We cannot form a correct notion of being as long as the mind does not make the effort to conceive it in the pure state, free of all connection with an added essence and sufficient to itself, without the addition of even a subject to support it and constitute a being with it. Words are hopeless, but we can think correctly what they fail to say well. Language reaches its extreme limit when the metaphysician dares to say that God is not really a being (*ens*) but pure being itself (*ipsum purum esse*).

Now we can conceive a finite being more clearly as composed of that which it is and a participation, by way of effect, in pure subsistent being. In us, being must be really other than essence because there is a being that is nothing but Being. Undoubtedly the direct consideration of finite being is enough to demonstrate its contingency, but here it is a question of the metaphysical structure itself of this contingent being. For all Christian theologies profess the contingency of finite creatures, but only one discovers the root of this contingency within them in the impossibility of the act that makes them exist to be Being purely and simply. All the basic theses of metaphysics come together here, for that which is, but is not Being, would not subsist for a moment without the immediate presence of the creative essence. The universe is composed of essences, no one of which is Being, but they are all beings because they exist and endure outside nothingness as effects of Him Who Is.

This doctrine has a metaphysical sobriety of astonishing grandeur. Many reproach it for not speaking enough to the heart, but they do not know what they are saying. For the heart to speak, or for us to speak to it, it must first exist. Even keeping within the order of affectivity and feeling – an order so legitimate in itself – what heart should not be content to know that it is so imbued with the divine power that it is nothing but its effect? Is there a closer dependence on a cause than to be an effect that depends on it for its very being? It is on this account that we live, move, and have being in Him.[7] God has only to stop willing us for us to cease to exist. The devotion would indeed be poor that failed to do justice to the feeling of this dependence, which, far from excluding those of heart and will, includes them and is their foundation. This is truly the greatest of all dependences. Within finite being, God keeps vigil with his power: the pure presence of Being to a being, which is *ens* only in virtue of *Esse*.

This metaphysics of being, moreover, is far from excluding a metaphysics of love, for why does God will nature and the human race except that he loves them? These reflections have their place, and when they arise they lose nothing by resting on a view of the world and God that is their foundation. God dwells in the very essence of the universe in which the Christian lives. Failing to understand that, we are in danger of missing the meaning of the central theses of theology, including those that directly govern the Master's teaching on the cooperation of God with the activity of creatures and on the economy of grace itself.

We could not make too great or too frequent an effort to meditate on the meaning of conclusions whose value diminishes to the point of disappearing when we fail to give them their full significance. God *is in* everything because he *acts in* everything, and wherever a being acts, there it exists: *Ubicumque operatur aliquid, ibi est* [ST 1.8.1 sed contra]. God's effect in a being is being, which he bestows because he himself Is. He creates and conserves this effect in things as long as they endure, as the sun causes light in the air as long as it is day. As long, then, as a thing has being,

7. [See Acts 17:28.]

God must be present to it, depending on the way it has being. Each of the other perfections has its value, but it would be nothing without being. Moreover, God is first present to his creature at its very center, he touches the being in its very core: *Unde oportet quod Deus sit in omnibus rebus, et intime* (So God must exist in all things, and most intimately: *ST* 1.8.1).

Such is the nature of this theology of causality, based on the theology of the act of being. Nothing could be more simple: By his essence God exists in all things inasmuch as he is present to them as the cause that gives them being: *Est in omnibus per essentiam, inquantum adest omnibus ut causa essendi* (*ST* 1.8.3). The other truths about the universe are important, but all of them come after this one, since God is present wherever there is being, and where God is not there is nothing. We must form the habit of reflecting on these truths, first on each of them in itself, then all together in the very process in which they give rise to each other, beginning with the proper name of God. Only then does the universe itself begin to reveal its secret, and no longer only why it is but what it is.

Being and Essences

... ex diverso modo essendi constituuntur diversi gradus entium (*Summa contra Gentiles* 1.50.7).[1]

The existence of the universe is unintelligible without the existence of God, but once reason has established that God is the pure act of being, it is no less perplexed to explain the existence of the universe. The universe needs God, but God does not need the universe. How can we conceive the possibility of something other than Being, once it has been affirmed that in itself it is infinite act?

We must not expect a clear and simple answer to this question, not only because it concerns being, but also because it bears on the mystery of the divine freedom. It is one more reason not to lose sight of the correct understanding of the question. Our inquiry begins with the world of nature, of which the human race is a part, and because it requires a first cause of its existence philosophers have found five main ways leading to the existence of God. Whatever further difficulties we may fear, we cannot deny the existence of Being – pure, infinite, perfectly simple, and the cause of everything besides itself. Since this universe exists, its production by such a being is certainly possible. The problem that remains is to investigate the reasons for this possibility.

The difficulties to overcome are especially serious in a theology like the present one, in which the first cause transcends the order of essence. The question is how essences can emanate from being in which no identifiable essence is added to *esse* to form a composition with it. When the question is put in this way, we see the direction in which we should look for the answer. If God is posited in the realm of essence, even at its summit, it would

1. ["... the grades of being are established from the diverse mode of existing."]

become very difficult, if not impossible, to find a place outside God for a world of creatures. Nothing can be added to, or subtracted from, the infinite, so that to Leibniz' statement, "There is only one God, and this God suffices,"[2] we could add the comment: and he is self-sufficient. But here we are starting from the notion of a God completely transcending the order of essences, which includes all creatures, from which we can conclude that no problem of addition or subtraction will arise between it and the beings it creates. *Entia* and *Esse* are strictly incommensurable. An illusion of the imagination creates pseudo-problems here that should be avoided.

Going deeper to the root of the question, reason is quite readily convinced that this is one of those difficulties in which metaphysics of clear and distinct ideas have no chance of finding satisfaction. Since the mind feeds on quidditative concepts, whose objects are essences, it cannot formulate in satisfactory language a relation between two terms, one of which is an essence and the other something beyond essence. The mind certainly conceives the act of being, but its conception of it is not a quidditative concept – the only one that would satisfy it because it alone lends itself to being defined. In dealing with the problem of the relation of essence to existence, the mind should accordingly resign itself at the outset to conclusions whose content cannot be completely represented. The unrepresentability of being in us is like the shadow cast by the unrepresentability of God.

We are left, then, with trying to find out how essence can come from that which transcends essence, while absorbing it in being. A contemporary philosopher has criticized metaphysicians of old for lingering over the problem of a being (*das Seiende*) without clearly grappling with that of being (*das Sein*).[3] Perhaps we have misunderstood the exact meaning of the criticism, for in our view the truth would rather seem to be that the most profound metaphysicians, from Plato to Thomas Aquinas and up

2. [Leibniz, *Monadology* 39, in *The Monadology and Other Writings*, trans. Robert Latta (London and New York: Oxford University Press, 1925), p. 239.]

3. [The reference is to Martin Heidegger. For Gilson's views on his philosophy see above p. 51 with n9.]

to our own time, have felt the need of going beyond the level of essence to reach that of the origin and cause of essence. Whatever may be the case with others, the metaphysics of *esse* is the typical instance of an ontology that expressly refuses to remain on the level of a being and presses forward to that of being, in which a being originates. True, once the metaphysician is there, he very seldom avoids speaking of being except in the language of a being, but those who reproach him for it do exactly the same thing. We would say they make the same mistake, if it were one. But it is not a mistake. The only error is to proclaim that, from now on, a serious start will be made to speak of *Sein*, or else to say that there would be lots of time to speak of it. The mind has only one language – that of essence. Nothing can be said of what lies beyond essence, except that it is and that it is the source of everything else. But it is necessary to know it and to say it, because to take essence for being is one of the most serious causes of error that threaten metaphysics. The metaphysician reaches the culmination of his reflection the moment he can no longer conceive a being except as a participation of being, which itself is incapable of being grasped except as involved in the essence of the being of which it is the act.

No matter under what aspect the problem is viewed, it seems impossible to escape the conclusion that essence is a lessening, a distention, and as it were a scattering of being. As long as we are in the presence of something that *has* being, we are below the level of being itself. For there can only be one single being as being; and since everything that is only a *certain being*, or that *has* being, is defined by its essence, the emanation of beings from being (*emanatio totius esse universalis* [see *ST* 1.45.1.]) would take place by way of a descent. What is difficult, and perhaps possible only imperfectly, is to understand the nature of the operation, grasped in some fashion at its source, that takes place at the moment when the first essence is separated from its cause, which is the pure act of *esse*.

The solution of the problem is usually based on the notion of the divine intellect, the realm of the Ideas, which are themselves the archetypes of essences. The solution is undoubtedly correct, and it can be justified by the express teaching of St. Thomas, following St. Augustine, on the nature of the divine ideas. But it is hardly an exaggeration to say that at bottom everything St.

Thomas said about the Ideas was in his view one more concession made to the language of a philosophy that was not really his own. No doubt it was also the recognition of St. Augustine's authority in theology.

In fact, the treatment of the problem and its discussion in *Contra Gentiles* (1.44–71) consigns the notion of a divine idea to the background. It appears briefly in chapters 51 and 54, where it is a question how a plurality of known objects can be in the divine intellect without destroying its unity, but St. Thomas mentions it only as a device used by St. Augustine to "save to some extent the opinion of Plato." The latter, says St. Thomas, placed the Ideas outside God, as self-subsistent, intelligible forms, in order to avoid introducing composition in the divine intellect. But this avoids one difficulty only to raise several others. In the first place, since God must then acquire his knowledge of objects other than his essence, his perfection would depend on beings other than himself, which is impossible. Moreover, since he is the cause of everything that is not his essence, these intelligible forms must be caused by God; and as he could not cause them without knowing them, his knowledge of them cannot depend on them but solely on himself. No matter how you look at it, it would not be an adequate solution to posit Ideas outside God in order to account for his knowledge of things. For God to know the forms of things, they must be in the divine intellect itself. Hence the Platonic solution of the problem does not work. The *Summa contra Gentiles* does not seem to have thought it necessary to make use of the Platonic notion of an Idea no matter how it is understood.

In fact, St. Thomas has no need of Ideas, for he can explain the truth of this matter without recurring to any notion that does not flow necessarily from his own principles or that is not identical with one of them. God is the prime mover. Whether we think of him as moving himself or as completely immovable, he must have knowledge. In both cases God moves as the object of desire and therefore insofar as he is known, and what he moves could not know unless he himself, who is the first being, has knowledge. But we immediately come back to the great principle of the divine simplicity. Understanding is related to the intellect as being is related to essence. Now being is God's essence. Therefore God's intellect is his essence, which is his being. Let St. Thomas speak for himself; it would be hard to outdo him in brevity: *Quicquid enim est in Deo est divina essentia. Intelligere ergo Dei est divina essentia, et divinum esse, et ipse Deus: nam Deus est sua essentia et suum esse* (Now, whatever is in God is the divine essence. Therefore God's act of understanding is the divine essence, and the divine being, and God himself; for God is his essence and his being [CG 1.45.2]).

What place do Ideas have in a doctrine like this? John Duns Scotus will make the pertinent observation that a theologian could give a very good account of the truth of God's knowledge of things without mentioning the notion of an idea.[4] It is at least as true in the doctrine of St. Thomas. Indeed, why claim there are ideas in God? To explain how he knows creatures *by means of them*? But God knows by his intellect, which is his essence, which is his *esse*. As St. Thomas emphasizes, if you require that all knowledge take place through an intelligible species, the essence of God is his intelligible species: *impossibile est quod in ipso sit aliqua species intelligibilis praeter ipsius essentiam ... . Non igitur intelligit per aliquam speciem quae non sit sua essentia* (It is impossible that there be in God an intelligible species other than his essence ... . Therefore God does not understand through a species that is not his essence: CG 1.46.5 and 6).

This leads to the astonishing conclusion that, if you wish to speak of intelligible species in connection with the divine knowledge, you can only attribute one of them to him. In one of St. Thomas's clearest analyses of the act of knowing (CG 1.53.4), he recalls that the intellect, having first been informed by a species coming from the known object, then in its act of knowing forms within itself an intelligible species of this object, and finally by means of this species produces a sort of *intention* of the same object. This *intention* is its intelligible notion (*ratio*), which the definition signifies. Accordingly the known intention, or formed notion, is the end of the act of understanding which began with the intelligible species. Consequently, the intellect is informed by a sensible object and its species; it itself forms an intelligible

---

4. [Duns Scotus, *De primo principio* 4.10, ed. and trans. as *The 'De primo principio' of John Duns Scotus* by Evan Roche (St. Bonaventure, New York; Louvain: Nauwelaerts, 1949), pp. 146 and 147.]

species; then, impregnated by this species, it forms the intelligible notion of the object, that is, its intention.

The only way we can think of the divine knowledge is to begin with what we know of our own. We will say, then, that God also knows things by an act of his intellect, and that his intellect knows them by means of an intelligible species which enables him to form a notion of them. In God's case, however, the intellect is his essence. For the same reason (the perfect simplicity of God), the act of the divine intellect is identical with that intellect and it itself is identical with the divine essence. Finally (always for the same reason), the intelligible species, the formal principle of the act of knowing, is identical in God with the intellect and its act. These are themselves identical with his essence. And since in the final analysis God's essence is identical with his being, in God being and knowing are one and the same: *intelligere Dei est ejus esse.*

You will notice, as a subject for lengthy reflection, the decisive role played here once again by the primary notion of the God of Exodus. If God knew by means of an intelligible species distinct from his essence, *it would be through something other than his essence* (CG 1.46.6), so strictly exact are the successive reductions to *esse* demanded by theological reasoning: *Si igitur intelligeret (Deus) per aliquam speciem quae non sit sua essentia, esset per aliquod aliud a sua essentia, quod est impossibile* (Therefore if God understood through a species that was not his essence, it would be through something other than his essence, which is impossible). But at the same time this shows us how little need this doctrine has for the notion of "divine ideas." Thomistic theology speaks the language of Aristotle, not that of Plato. Besides, it says things in the language of Aristotle that are scarcely Aristotelian, in the present case about intelligible species. If one insists on speaking of God, Aristotle will be made to say that, since whatever God knows he knows through his essence, he knows everything through one single and unique "known intention," which is the divine Word, from a single and unique intelligible species, which is the divine essence itself (CG 1.53.5). In short, if one is determined to use the language of Ideas, it must be said that there is only one, namely God.

In fact, nothing is needed but God, for he exists, he is his own self- knowledge, and because that knowledge at the same time extends to all his actual and possible effects, it is literally true to say that the knowledge God has of his essence, or is, includes that of all the beings he causes or can cause. Therefore God in his very being is the intelligible notion of each individual: *ipse (est) propria ratio singulorum* (*CG* 1.54.4). And because in this crossroads of great metaphysical themes it is impossible to grasp one without including the others, let us not allow this occasion to slip by without casting a glance at what the divine knowledge tells us about the structure of beings. Because the divine essence is absolute existence, it includes the infinity of possible forms, each of which, insofar as it itself is, is a perfection containing no imperfection save that of failing to be true being: *secundum quod deficit a vero esse* (*CG* 1.54.4). Essences are finite and deficient approximations of the pure act of *esse*.

If St. Thomas had no other partners in dialogue than the Gentiles, to whom he addressed that first *Summa*, he would no doubt have stopped there, for he spoke to them in their own language, which was that of Aristotelianism, while at the same time making it his own whenever he felt free to express himself directly and in a sort of self- dialogue. He will never return to this doctrine in any of his other works to deny any part of it or even simply to modify it. The *Summa theologiae* 1.14, takes up the whole doctrine again and even develops it: God knows, God knows himself, God comprehends himself, God's knowledge is his very substance, in other words his being: *Unde cum ipsa sua essentia sit etiam species intelligibilis, ut dictum est* (1.14.2), *ex necessitate sequitur quod ipsum ejus intelligere sit ejus essentia et ejus esse* (Therefore, since his essence itself is also his intelligible species, as we have said, it necessarily follows that his act of understanding is his essence and his being; 1.14.4).

However, he seems to open up a new perspective in the next question, *De Ideis* (*ST* 1.15). Now that we have treated of God's knowledge, says St. Thomas, we still have to take ideas into account. We can wonder why. Having already based the divine knowledge of individuals on what should in every sense be its ultimate foundation (*ipsum Esse*), why add to the doctrine that sort of enclave devoted to the Ideas? Are there Ideas? Are there many of them or only one? Are there Ideas for everything God knows?

The answer is given in the *sed contra* of the first of the three articles. Yes, we *must* posit ideas in the divine mind because, according to St. Augustine, they are so important that unless one

understands them he cannot be wise (*Lib. 83 Quaest.*, q. 46).[5]
Clearly, we are in theology, where Augustine wields great authority. Bonaventure, among many others, places Augustinian exemplarism at the very core of theological truth, as the necessary condition of a Christian ontology, epistemology, and ethics. By his
Ideas God becomes for us *causa subsistendi, ratio intelligendi, et ordo
vivendi* (the cause of our subsisting, the reason of our understanding, and the order of our living).[6] Are we going to exclude or
ignore this doctrine sanctioned by the great name of Augustine?[7]
Surely not. A place must be made for it, while showing that,
whether necessary or not, it is authentic.

Let us take note that there is no question here of adding one
more piece to a sort of philosophical mosaic. St. Thomas had a
different object in view. Being a theologian, he sets himself the
task of showing how the Augustinian doctrine of Ideas can be
tied in with the strictest philosophical truth, which itself does not
give way an inch. Thomas is here taking Augustinism in tow. It
is easy to see this from the perspective of the Augustinian-Platonic
realm presented so clearly in Question 15, *De Ideis* [*ST* 1.15.] An
idea means a form. Forms are either in their natural state in
things, or in the speculative intellect as likenesses of the forms of
natural things, or finally in the practical intellect as models of
things to be made. There is the form of a house; there is this form
of a house known by the intellect of the one who sees it; and
there is the form of the same house preconceived by the mind of
the architect who is going to build it. St. Thomas makes the
happy suggestion that the word "idea" should *rather* be reserved
for forms in the third mode of existence. He is well aware that
absolutely speaking ideas cannot be attributed to God without
ascribing to him speculative as well as practical ideas. The Intelligible Sun of Plato, Plotinus, and Augustine had thoughts as well

5. [Augustine, *De diversis quaestionibus* 46 ("De Ideis").1, ed. Almut
Mutzenbecher CCL 44A: 70.]

6. [Bonaventure, *Collationes de septem donis Spiritus Sancti* 8.15–16,
in *Opera omnia*, 10 vols. (Quaracchi: Ex typographia Collegi S. Bonaventurae, 1882–1902), 5: 496–497.]

7. [Augustine, *De civitate Dei* 8.4, ed. Bernard Dombart and
Alphonse Kalb CCL 47: 220.53–54.]

as plans. St. Thomas knows even better that his own doctrine contains in a higher way the truth of Augustinism and that it can do without it. God knows perfectly his own essence (which is his *esse*). Hence he knows it in every way it can be known:

> Now it can be known not only as it is in itself, but also as it can be participated by creatures according to some manner of likeness. Now every creature has its own species, according to the special way it participates in the likeness of the divine essence. Consequently, as God knows his essence as imitable in this way by a creature of that species, he knows it (that is, his essence) as the particular notion and idea of that creature; and similarly with other creatures (*ST* 1.15.2).

In other words, we can call a divine idea the knowledge the divine essence has of its possibility of being imitated by a particular finite essence. So the Augustinian doctrine of ideas is true. But we knew this beforehand, for, since God's intellect is his very essence, it is clear that his essence and the knowledge he has of it are identical. So it is one and the same thing for God to be and to be the ideas of all actual and possible finite creatures. We are not saying that the term "Idea" has no specific meaning, but this meaning does not concern the divine essence itself. God has no idea of God; the plurality of ideas known by God is only a plurality of natures in things: *idea non nominat divinam essentiam inquantum est essentia* (an Idea does not denote the divine essence insofar as it is an essence: *ST* 1.15.2 ad 1m). Thus St. Thomas does not adapt his own thought to that of St. Augustine, but he welcomes the latter's truth and makes room for it. Even in doing so he firmly maintains his own, and far from disavowing question 14, question 15 confirms it: God is like all things in the same way that an architect is like all the houses he builds, except in this respect, that in God there is no distinction between being himself and being the model of possible creatures: *Deus secundum essentiam suam est similitudo omnium rerum* (through his essence God is the likeness of all things). If you wish, you can call this essential exemplarity of God an idea; it will not remain less identical with the divine essence itself: *Unde idea in Deo nihil est aliud quam Dei essentia* (So an idea in God is nothing else than God's essence: *ST* 1.15.1 ad 3m).

Let us pause again to recognize here the theologian in the exercise of his proper function. As the "common sense" receives and judges the data of the external senses, the theologian accepts, relates, and judges the data of the various philosophies. If the theologian is content to pass judgment solely on the basis of whether these philosophies are in fact compatible with the truth of faith, he correctly fulfils his office without doing anything else, but it is still important. St. Thomas's work as a theologian goes much further. What sets him apart is that the judgment of the theologian draws its inspiration not only from the rule of faith, but at the same time from a philosophical truth more profound than that appealed to by the theologies it replaces. Progress in philosophy and progress in theology are so closely tied together that in fact they coincide. But progress is accomplished through the work of the theologian: the understanding of being benefits from the understanding of faith.

This attempt to conceive the whole of reality – if we can speak this way without sounding ridiculous – somewhat similar to the way God knows himself, in the end encounters the darkness of the philosophical mystery *par excellence*: the problem *de rerum originatione radicali* (of the radical coming into being of things). This mystery, moreover, must be situated exactly. For one mystery would consist in knowing why God willed things; but this depends on the secret of the most supremely free act imaginable. Prior to it (philosophically speaking) there is the mystery implied in the possibility of what is meant in general by the word "things." For God is not a thing; neither is he a group of things. He *is* absolutely. How is it possible, then, that there be something that is a being, or beings, which are not identical with being itself, that is, with Him Who Is?

Metaphysics reaches the end of its journey at this point, as is evident from the fact that it has recourse to metaphor. *Similitudo, exemplar, imitatio*: all these words direct the mind to a truth that it could not formulate exactly, for after all, in what sense and in what way does that whose being is to have a specifically definite essence resemble that whose whole essence is to be? Even more paradoxically, but in the language of St. Thomas himself, how can that whose being is pure *esse* be the exemplary likeness of a multitude of beings, none of which is its own *esse*?

Platonism, especially that of Plotinus, opens up the easiest approaches to this greatest of problems. No doctrine more clearly reveals the connection between the notions of being and intelligibility than that of the *Enneads*.[8] The One is at the summit of the hierarchy of substantive Principles (*substances-principes*), but nothing could be said of the absolute One, not even that it exists, for this would amount to affirming that it is being and no longer the One. It cannot even be said that the One is the One, for if we think of the One twice we make it two. In brief, the One is ineffable. We cannot form any proposition about it which would not destroy it, and this is true of the One itself. Undoubtedly the One is not unconscious. Quite the contrary, it is at the peak of immateriality and knowledge. But it does not know by means of propositions, and it could not form any about itself which would make it *know what it is*. The One is beyond "that which," and since there is nothing that it is, it is beyond being. Speaking strictly and properly, the One *is not*.

Being, then, appears below the One. With deep insight, Plotinus has being begin along with, and at the same time as, knowledge of Ideas, for we can only truly say that being is when we can say what it is. That is why the second substantive Principle, coming immediately after the One, is the Intelligence (*Nous*), which, precisely because it is knowledge, is being. The Intelligence is not the One, but it is the knowledge of the One, if not in itself, which transcends knowledge, at least under the form of all its possible participations. As known, these possible participations are called Ideas. Thus it is with the Intelligence, the realm of Ideas, that we truly arrive at the domain of being. Recalling this doctrine, which he had found in the *Liber de causis*, St. Thomas will astutely turn it to his own advantage when he quotes with pleasure the proposition he made famous: *prima rerum creatarum est esse*. The first thing coming after the One (which is itself first) is being.[9]

8. [For Gilson's views on Plotinus's philosophy see *Being and Some Philosophers*, 2nd ed. (Toronto: Pontifical Institute of Mediaeval Studies, 1952), pp. 20–29.]

9. [See Aquinas, *Expositio super librum 'De causis'* 4, ed. H.D. Saffrey, Textus philosophici friburgenses 4/5 (Freiburg: Société philosophique; Louvain: Nauwelaerts, 1954), p. 26.]

This inseparability of being and intelligibility, then, comes from the fact that nothing begins to be as long as we cannot know and say that it is. At the same time we enter a realm in which thought feels at home. After the One, the ineffable, and the indefinable, there simultaneously follow the many, the expressible, and the definable. The mind at once lays hold of its proper object, the *ratio* of the known being, that is, the concept of the being formed by the intellect and signified by the name: *Ratio enim quam significat nomen, est conceptio intellectus de re significata per nomen* (*ST* 1.13.4). Indeed, multiplicity presupposes distinction, which presupposes delimitation or "definition" both in being and knowledge. Thus the concept designated by the name signifies, so to speak, one definite ontological unity among others, which are not it and which it is not.

We learn a lesson from this Plotinian experience with the notion of the One. Starting from the One, the many can be reached only in the form of distinct, intelligible Ideas. Unless they are conceived as such, these intelligible forms *are* not. They are not, then, *beings*. In short, the intelligibility of these forms is a necessary intermediary between unity, which transcends being, and being, which is found only in multiplicity.

We cannot picture the process. If we try to imagine it, we think of a sort of metaphysical explosion of the One, shattering itself in Ideas, but nothing of the sort happens. The One remains one, indifferent to that proliferation of images of itself in which it is not involved, because its unity is not that of a number whose sum can be obtained by adding or subtracting units. The One remains aloof from, and unaffected by that multiplication. The many is made up of fragments of a unity which is not that of their sum total. The old metaphor of the image is still the best here, for an infinity of reflections in a set of mirrors adds nothing to the substance of the object they represent. The object itself, moreover, is not made up of images. The object and its image do not belong to the same genus, so that the images are produced from it without taking away any of its being, and they can disappear without its being changed.

Why, then, do we become involved in these unsolvable problems? Since we are confronted with a multitude made up of individual beings which the intellect can conceive, why add to it the One, whose relation to the many is so hard to understand? Simply because the opposition of the one and the many is not a mental fiction; it is given in the many itself, since we can only conceive it as a sort of unity. This holds good for both conceptual and real being. Let us take any concept as an example, "man" for instance. We shall find it made up of distinct elements united by the copula of the judgment: man is a rational animal. In reality itself, a being only endures as long as it remains one with itself. As Leibniz liked to repeat, it is the same thing to be *one* being and to be one *being*.[10] Hence being is given in unity. It is only possible and conceivable by that element that generates the concept which itself escapes conceptualization.

St. Thomas always showed a lively interest in the Platonic dialectic of the one and the many because in his view it prefigured that of being and essence. In a Christian philosophy, born of a rational reflection on the word of God, the first Principle is not the One but Being. Like the One, being escapes definition. It is a commonplace that the notion of being cannot be precisely defined because, being first, it necessarily includes all the terms one could use to define it. And yet, outside of being there is only nothing. Hence the mind constantly uses as the first principle a notion that it understands but that eludes the grasp of reason in its reasoning function. Nothing can be said of being, even finite being, except that it is the act by which a being is or exists. Everything happens as though created *esse* shared in the mysterious character of the creative cause; and indeed, to conceive finite *esse* in itself and in the pure state would be a contradictory undertaking; it would be trying to conceive God.

We are here at the origin of all the difficulties raised by the notion of essence and existence in finite being. Those who raise them are not wrong, for they are real. Rather, we would accuse the defenders of the doctrine of indiscretion or rudeness if they wanted to prove to their opponents that these difficulties exist only in their imagination. The purpose of metaphysical reflection is not to eliminate the mystery of being, but rather to recognize its place and to attempt a first approach to it. We must realize

10. [*The Leibniz–Arnauld Correspondence,* ed. and trans. H.T. Mason, with an introduction by G.H.R. Parkinson (New York: Barnes & Noble; Manchester: Manchester University Press, 1967), p. 121.]

above all that the notion of finite being is only incompletely comprehensible, and not only for us but also in itself, for God himself could not create by itself an act of being at once finite and self-subsistent. Being, pure and unique, is God. Finite being can only subsist as determined by something which is not pure being. So it is necessary that finite being be composed precisely insofar as it is finite being, and that composition is necessarily of *esse* and an element other than *esse*. Those who object to that composition are wrong to attack the doctrine; being itself is responsible for it, for this is how it is made. But those who are astonished that anyone has difficulty with it are not themselves very reasonable, for if there is nothing outside of being except nothingness, with what could *esse* enter into composition except with being? But a composition of being with being does not seem to be a clear notion; for we can easily understand that one being is added to another to form a being of a different species than its components, but it is unthinkable that being must be added to being in order that being itself be possible. Being not only accompanies all our representations; it precedes them and conditions them. While entering into the composition of everything, it itself could not be composed.

The objections of the Suarezians to the Thomistic metaphysics of finite being are unanswerable on the level of reason and quidditative being on which they are made. The mistake of many of their Thomist opponents is to accept the Suarezian notion of metaphysical knowledge and then wish to reject the Suarezian notion of being. If it be granted, with Suárez, that essence is being itself, how could it be united with anything whatsoever to make a being of it? This would be to make it what it already is. But it is not a matter of "refuting" the doctrine of Suárez. There is even no reason to do away with it, supposing it were possible, which is doubtful. Rather, the metaphysics of essences and quidditative concepts, far from being unintelligible, would be the natural metaphysics of the human mind, with its fondness for that *ratio intellecta* it forms with ease and on which it eagerly feeds: *conceptio intellectus de re significata per nomen*. It is good that the mind has at its disposal a metaphysics of essence, which is suitably called ontology. It is even better to have a metaphysics of being which, bravely plunging into the depths of mystery, sees at least enough of it to recognize its existence. However, the person who gets involved in it must not expect it to give him the satisfactions only afforded by the exercise of discursive reason working with clear and distinct ideas. It would be even less excusable to promise them to others, for it can be said of being, as it can be said of God, that in a sense not knowing it is the best way to know it. And indeed, what is *a being* if not the image of Him Who Is?

The metaphysician finds himself here in a situation similar to that of the Platonist; but instead of inquiring how the One can give birth to the many without dividing itself, he must try to understand how Being can cause beings without compromising its own simplicity. And just as the One of Plotinus begot those reflections of itself which are the Ideas, so also Being makes those created participations emanate from itself which are essences. In the two metaphysics the transcendence of the First Principle remains intact and secure. The many *is not* the One; no essence is He Who Is. Essence, then, must be a kind of "small change" of Being, as the many is the "small change" of the One. But because in the two cases it is a matter of realities of different orders, the One would never be reconstituted by joining together the infinity of Ideas, any more than Being would be reconstituted by gathering together in a bundle the infinity of essences. The One is not remade with the many nor Being with essences – which invites us to think of essence as a by-product of Being. It is the condition of the possibility of beings which are not the pure act of existing.

St. Thomas himself was not in a better position than we are to formulate this relation of essence to being within the heart of a being. In one sense this is a question of a relation of being to being, for if the essence itself did not belong to a being it would be nothing. But in another sense the essence does not belong to a being in exactly the same way that *esse* does. If this were not so, being infinite like *esse*, it would be God. We must concede, then, that essence indeed belongs to *esse*, but determined and delimited. Or rather, we must grant that essence is the determination, delimitation, restriction, and contraction of *esse*. This is what St. Thomas gives us to understand when he says that essence is a mode of being. For us the expression means a "way of being," and this is in fact its import. But the different "ways" of being are first of all, if we may use the expression, "measures" of being. Here we are surely resorting to a metaphor, for the qualitative differences among essences could not be taken literally as quantitative differences of being. It seems, however, that this is the best expression Thomas himself could come up with, and he liked it all the more because the Philosopher had suggested it when he said that essences are like numbers. Add one to a number, or subtract one, and you have different species of numbers, with properties as different as those of equality or inequality. Likewise, in the realm of beings, increase or diminish the participation of a being in being and you alter the species. Add life to mineral and you have a plant; add sensibility to life and you have an animal; and if reason is conferred on animal, the human species appears. Thus understood, essences are accordingly distinguished from each other as the measures of the quantity of being that constitutes and defines each species.

After that, there will be no surprise at the difficulties facing those who want to use some image to represent the relation of being to essence at the heart of a being. Being is there the proper effect of God, the participation (by way of effect) in pure *Esse* which is its cause. Hence being (*esse*) has the function of the first and supreme act in the complex metaphysical structure of a being. In fact, it is through *esse* that everything else is something real and can contribute to the constitution of a being (*ens*). True, a being is that which has being, but in a being the "that which" has no reality except through the being that it has. So nothing can equal in importance the role of being in a being, since without it there is nothing.

A frequent and long-standing objection is that a living being is more perfect than a being that is only a being, and a sentient being is more perfect than one that is only living, and a being endowed with reason is more perfect than one with only sense knowledge. From this the conclusion is drawn that, far from being what is most perfect in a being, being is there as in potency to all the essential forms that determine it. No objection shows more clearly the fundamental illusion that obscures the whole problem. For it is indeed certain that the least determined being, that is, the one closest to prime matter, is less perfect than the beings whose essences are arranged in stages above it according to the hierarchy of their forms. This is what has just been said: essences are distinguished as the quantities of being that constitute them. A rational being is accordingly more than a being that is only living, and so on, but this entire hierarchy presupposes the being of the elements that constitute it. The comparison of different degrees of being is possible only because being first of all makes them realities. We should not ask, then, if non-living being is more or less perfect than living being, and so on, but rather if the being of anything whatsoever is more or less perfect than its non-being. When the question is raised in these terms, the answer is inevitable: what is most perfect in a being is being, to which nothing else can be compared because outside of it there is nothing.

The illusion we should constantly guard against is to think that the perfection of anything whatsoever, even that of essence, can be placed in opposition to that of being, which is the unique perfection, thanks to which the others, as they attain the status of reality, owe the possibility of being compared with it. The mind wavers here between two judgments, for on the one hand an essence is necessarily required for the possibility of the existence of a finite being, but on the other hand the act of being is necessarily required for an essence, which of itself is only possible, to reach the actual reality that posits it outside nothingness. There is, then, a reciprocal causality, but within being and not exercised on the same level of perfection, for the *actus essendi* causes the very being of a thing, while the essence or form, for its part, contributes only the mode in which the finite act of being can be exercised.

St. Thomas expresses this truth when he asserts that in a finite being, being is the act of all acts and the perfection of all perfections [*QDP* 7.2 ad 9m], for its modality, which is essence, only exists through it. Bañez states the same truth in the passage of his commentary[11] in which, coining for the occasion the verb "to imperfect" as the opposite of "to perfect," he says that the act of being is "imperfected" (*imperficitur*) by the essence. The expression makes sense because, if the act of being *without the added essence* is actually posited outside the mind, it is precisely the infinite act of being, which is God. In a doctrine in which God's name is He Who Is, the primacy of the act of being in a finite being follows directly from the absolute transcendence of pure being.

11. [Domingo Bañez, *Scholastica commentaria in primam partem 'Summae theologicae' s. Thomae Aquinatis* 1.3.4, ed. Luis Urbano, Biblioteca de Tomistas españoles 8 (Madrid and Valencia: Editorial F.E.D.A., 1934), p. 141a.]

Important consequences follow from this for the general interpretation of a metaphysics based on this notion of being. Clearly,
it cannot be thought of as a philosophy of essence, for it is the act
of being (*esse*) that plays the role of first act and first perfection in
it, essence itself being only in potentiality to it. No less clearly, it
cannot be thought of as a philosophy of existence in a spirit similar to that of contemporary existentialisms, in which existence is
opposed to essence as its contrary. Everything affirmed by the
metaphysics of essence remains true in the philosophy whose
principle we have just defined, except the illusion that makes
them posit essence as the supreme act and perfection, which
amounts to ascribing to it the place and the role reserved for *esse*.

How could we underrate or slight essence? Undoubtedly it is
of little value when compared with God. In him, an essence is
only an idea, the knowledge of a possible mode of participation
in the pure act of being by a being which, not being God, is
infinitely inferior to him. But the contrary is true of essence
compared to nothingness, for the only other possibilities, apart
from being God himself, are to be a being or not to be. Now, if a
being is infinitely distant from being, so too in its own way is
nothingness infinitely distant from being, since the creative act,
which is the proper mode of the divine causality, is alone capable
of bridging it.

We shall never sing too loudly, then, the praise of essences –
those mirrors in which is reflected in an infinite number of different ways the simple perfection of the transcendent pure act of
being. Their intelligibility, order, goodness, and beauty are those
of the whole created universe, actual or possible. What is distinc-
tive of essence – the finite mode of participation in being – is to
make possible the existence of a *natura rerum* which is neither
nothing nor God. That is why we have presented it as the ontological condition of the very possibility of a reality that is not
divine. Victorious over nothingness by the creator's free will, such
a universe is composed of beings that are neither essences without
existence nor existences without essences, but rather acts of being
measured by the essences on which they themselves confer existence. It is a universe of great beauty, sacred in its very being, the
intimate abode of the efficacy of the divine omnipotence, the inexhaustible food for philosophical and theological reflection, whose
very nature links it to spirituality.

Must we give a name to this kind of metaphysics? But it is not a kind of metaphysics; it is metaphysics itself at the extreme point of penetration into the nature of being. In any case it could be called neither an essentialism (concerned with essence without being) nor an existentialism (concerned with being without essence). To give it a name, it should be called an "ontism"; but this would not get us very far, because the term would simply mean "philosophy of being." In fact, everything is either the being of Him Who Is, or the mode of being of a being measured by its essence and created by the divine efficacy: *nihil praeter ipsum est nisi ab ipso* (Everything besides God derives its being from him: CG 2.15.1).

Being, Act, and End

Quod non habet esse actu, appetit esse actu (*Quaestiones de veritate*, 22.1 ad 4m).[1]

Words change their meaning as a result of the evolution of metaphysical doctrines. "Existence" today has implications different from those of *existentia* in former times, above all, for example, in a doctrine like that of Bañez, in which the meaning of the word did not in any way differ from that of the verb or verbal substantive *esse*. In order to understand the doctrine, then, we must direct our efforts to rediscovering the precise meaning of the language that expresses it. What exactly is that created, finite, concrete being that we call a being (*ens*)? What role does its act of being (*esse*) play in it? Finally, what is the relation between this act and the activities that reveal its fundamental dynamism? These are the principal notions with which our philosophical reflection must now come to grips.

Finite being (*esse*) is the proper effect of the creative act, but we have seen that it could not be created separately. It can only be concreated with and in the essence of which it is the act, but from which it receives its measure. In short, it can only be concreated with a being (*ens*). The technical word for a being is "substance." Thus it is the same thing to create *beings* or to create *substances*, for what is not strictly a substance can only exist by and in substances. Everything else, therefore, is concreated with and in substance – the only kind of finite being that truly deserves the name of being because it alone is able to exist.

This is the origin of the usual definition of substance: *ens per se*, a being through itself; or, in other words, existing or capable of existing through itself alone, in opposition to *ens per aliud*, or

---

1. ["What does not actually have being desires to be actually."]

an accident, which is incapable of existing apart and except in a substance. Moreover, this is why it is commonly said that a substance possesses *esse*, that is to say, a being of its own, but that the being of an accident is reducible to "being in" a substance. An accident exists only of and by the being of a substance; it has no being of its own, distinct from the being of a substance: *accidentis esse est inesse* (the being of an accident is to-be-in: *ST* 1.28.2).

In itself this notion of substance is correct, but not the form in which it is usually expressed. There is an *ens per se*, but there is only one of them, namely God. There are other reasons for avoiding the use of this definition. In the formula *ens per se*, a being (*ens*) plays the role of the genus and *per se* that of the difference. But being is not a genus, because all genera and differences are included in being. So we cannot conceive substance as the species of what is *per se* in the genus *ens*. If we absolutely must define substance – although it is the widest genus – we must rather say that it is "that to whose quiddity it is owing not to be in something": *substantia est res cujus quidditati debetur esse non in aliquo* (*QDP* 7.3 ad 4m).

This way of defining substance is a natural consequence of the notion of finite being made famous by Avicenna and deepened by Thomas Aquinas.[2] The problem here is to define a certain mode of existing: that which belongs to substance. So it is the essence, the *modus essendi*, which is here at stake. If the essence in question is such that it is capable of bearing by itself an act of existing, the corresponding being is a substance. On the contrary, if the essence in question is incapable of bearing by itself an act of existing, the corresponding being is an accident. The essence of a stone is that of a possible substance. The essence of a color, or of any other sensible quality, could not exercise its own distinct act of existing; so it is only the essence of an accident. St. Thomas always gave primacy of place to this more exact

2. [For the notion of substance see Gilson, *The Christian Philosophy of St. Thomas Aquinas,* with a catalogue of St. Thomas' works by I.T. Eschmann, trans. Laurence K. Shook (New York: Random House, 1956), pp. 29–39, and "Quasi Definitio Substantiae," in *St. Thomas Aquinas 1274–1974: Commemorative Studies,* ed. Armand Maurer, 2 vols. (Toronto: Pontifical Institute of Mediaeval Studies, 1974), 1: 111–129.]

definition of substance, and it is important that we make it our own. The definition of substance is not *ens per se*; rather, we must say of it: *quod habeat quidditatem cui conveniat esse non in alio* (that it has a quiddity to which it belongs to be not in another: *CG* 1.25.10). Moreover, this is why, properly speaking, God is not a substance, for he has no essence besides his *esse*. The only possible substances are finite and composed of essence and being. The word *substantia*, to speak precisely, signifies *essentiam cui competit sic esse, id est per se esse, quod tamen esse non est ipsa ejus essentia* (an essence to which it belongs to be in this way, namely, through itself, which being, however, is not its very essence: *ST* 1.3.5 ad 1m; see 3.77.1 ad 2m). In short, a substance is not being; it is always a being.

To this we must add that a substance is a being through the *esse* that makes it a being. In this sense the created *esse* is truly the cause of the being; but we should not imagine it to be like an efficient cause, whose activity would be to produce the actual existence of the finite being. If it were this kind of cause, it itself would first have to be an *ens* and exercise an activity. This is not the case with finite *esse*. Rather, we should think of it as a formal constitutive principle of a being; to be precise, as that through which the essence is a being. So we must break the structure of Aristotelianism, in which the essential form is the highest formal element, for here there is something still more formal than essence, and this is precisely *esse*, the constitutive principle of a being, which unites with the essence to constitute a substance. Being is that which is most formal in finite being, but its formality is not of the same order as that of essence, of which it is the act.

Finally, since this actuality of being is that of a substantial principle, it must not be conceived as an activity that would unfold, while displaying its efficacy over a period of time. An effect of God, and therefore a participation in the pure act of being, the finite *esse* subsists in the heart of a being as an act motionless and at rest: *aliquid fixum et quietum in ente* (something fixed and at rest in a being [*CG* 1.20.24]). Actual being is not correctly conceived as a becoming. We should not refuse to reduce it to essence only to mistake it for a kind of substantialized duration of which it would be the flux. Here metaphysical reflection is in danger of making a twofold error. One consists in reducing a being to an actualized essence. The other – in order to avoid this pitfall – dissolves essence into a constantly changing flux, or rather, considers it to be change itself. Being, rightly understood, is neither an inert ontological mass nor a becoming. Its immobility is that of an act analogous to that of the pure act of being, which, without having to change in order to become what it is (since it is being), is nevertheless the source of a becoming, in the course of which it displays its fecundity without itself being involved in it. Being is not movement, but it causes movement; and that it why it could not be completely described without adding a description of its activities.

As a matter of fact, these belong less to being than to a being. Once being has actualized essence, it has done everything it had to do, but it is not enough for an essence to be the essence of a being in order to be completely realized. On the contrary, by its essence a being is an active center of many different activities, whose specific purpose is to fulfill it in line with its own nature, to enable it to perfect its powers; in short, to make it become what it is.

These propositions are not intelligible on their own level. In order to understand them we must once again go back to the primary metaphysical notions from which they flow. The first of all these is the notion of being and not, as one is inclined to think, the notion of act. Act is understood by being and not vice versa. It is true that act and potency divide all being, but this is so precisely because act presupposes being, which itself is only being in act or being in potency. Act and potency are substantial modes (*QDP* 3.8 ad 12m), that is to say, ways of being or modalities of being. We are on the wrong track if we enter into metaphysics beginning with the notions of act and potency. The consequences of that initial mistake are fatal. On the contrary, we should begin with being, the primary notion to which we must refer all the others.

It is one and the same thing to be and to be in act. We see this clearly in the unique case of God who, inasmuch as he is being in its absolute purity (*ipsum purum esse*) is at the same time pure act. There is no place in Him Who Is for any "able to be," since he is everything he can be. Moreover, that is why we do not define God when we say he is pure act (*QDP* 7.3 ad 5m), for that supposed definition simply means that God is pure being, and, as we recall, when it is a question of God the meaning of the verb "is" escapes us. In short, if the divine being were the only being, there would be no occasion for using the word "act"; the word "being" would suffice.

The exact meaning of the word "act" can be more easily grasped in the case of a finite being, for this *is not* being but *has* it. Finite being is *a certain being*. So a question of more or less arises in its regard. First, if this being is compared to pure Being, which it can imitate more or less perfectly. Second, if what this being is, is compared to what it is capable of becoming, as we compare to the plan that a work brings into existence the part of it that is already completed. A human being, a rational animal, is more than a plant; among humans an educated mind is more than one uneducated, and so on for other finite beings. To the extent that one of these beings is, we say it is in act. On the contrary, we say it is in potency insofar as there is some distance between what it could be and is not. In this case there exists a degree of perfection of being, and this perfection is the exact measure of its act. On the other hand, the lack of the act of being constitutes and determines its potency and imperfection. It should be noted that potency is not opposed to being; on the contrary, it is being-in-potency. In short, it is a deficient mode of being, a failure to measure up to the degree of actuality of which that being is naturally capable. We should guard against conceiving act and potency as two forces with opposite meanings, for if potency in no way pertained to being it would be absolutely nothing. So there is nothing but a certain being, whose degree of actuality (that is to say, of being) is its degree of perfection.

We can easily understand now that finite being is active by nature and the cause of activities. The very fact that its perfection and actuality are limited makes it perfectible. It is not perfectible indefinitely and in every way, but in the manner and within the limits defined by its essence. What it is not, but is able to be if a cause gives it this additional actuality, also pertains to its being, act, and perfection. Consequently, it pertains to its goodness, because every being is good insofar as it is; and it is in a very special way its own goodness, since it is a possible increase in its own being. That is why every being loves being as a good, and it loves it under all its forms. In the first place it loves its own, making every effort to preserve it, to make it endure, and to defend it against the mortal dangers that threaten it. Besides its own being, every finite being also loves what complements its own in other beings and that can be incorporated in it. Finally, every being loves the beings it can give birth to or produce, for, being like their cause, they so to speak prolong and multiply it in substances and under new forms. A father, a workman, an artist, a man of action under all its forms, naturally take pleasure in their works, in the materials themselves needed to produce them; in short, in everything that can further their birth. The love of act under all its possible forms is nothing else than the love of being and its perfection.

Here the primary notions of metaphysics seem to merge and intermingle. Being is the actuality of everything: *esse est actualitas omnis rei*. Everything is perfect insofar as it is in act: *intantum est perfectum unumquodque, inquantum est actu*. It is clear, then, that each thing is good to the extent that it is: *intantum est aliquid bonum inquantum est ens* (*ST* 1.5.1). Lastly, since we have said that substance alone can exercise an act of being, it is as a substance that everything is properly a being in act, and not only in potency or by accident (ibid. ad 1m). Beginning with this notion of substantial being, we can just as easily recognize the notions governing the order of acting, of making, and in general of operating. Everything that is, is good insofar as it is being: *Omne quod est, inquantum est ens, necesse est esse bonum* (*CG* 2.41.5). Since the good is being insofar as it is desirable, everything loves its being, desires to conserve or perfect it, and undertakes the activities necessary for these ends, so that action is like a manifestation of being, which itself is act: *Omne agens agit inquantum est actu; inquantum vero est actu, unumquodque perfectum est* (Every agent acts insofar as it is in act; and insofar as it is in act, everything is perfect: *CG* 2.41.6). It amounts to the same thing to say that everything acts insofar as it is, or that it is in act, or that it is perfect (that is to say, lacking nothing, given the measure of its being), or that it is good. Activity, then, springs from being as from a formal or efficient cause, tending toward the good, which is only another word for being as a final cause. Thus the universe of finite beings ceaselessly acts and operates in order to acquire the being and goodness that it lacks; for even though each of them is good insofar as it is, it is not the same thing for it to be and to be goodness itself (*CG* 3.21.4).

How extraordinary a universe! So natural in itself, and at the same time so supernaturally Christian! Solid, permanent, created in time but for eternity, this world in which each nature is endowed with its own being and efficacy, nevertheless operates only through the divine efficacy, of which its being is the effect, and in view of God who, as he is its cause, is also its end.

Before giving further attention to this universe, it is well to have a clear idea of where we are going. We are not concerned here with the sciences of nature, their object, their methods or their own ends. Excellent in itself and independent in its own domain, science does not expect any properly scientific guidance from metaphysics. What we shall be concerned with and interpret in its very being is science itself, taken as a whole and along with its object. We must not expect a scientific explanation of the possibility of science. Metaphysics alone, whose object is being as being, can offer an answer to this question.

Every being acts in order to produce and to acquire some good that it lacks, that is, to develop and perfect itself both in its being and in its goodness. But God is the absolute being and good. So the purpose of all causal activity is to enable the being that exercises it to make itself more like God. We say "more like" because, however insignificant it may be, a being is the image of God to the extent to which it is. By augmenting its being through acquiring a higher perfection (that is, by actualizing a part of its potentiality), the substance increases its likeness to God. Whether it knows it or not, whether it wishes it or not, that is what it does. For even though everything, in each of its activities, strives to obtain some special good as its own particular end, at the same time and with the same act it pursues the further universal end of rendering itself more like God.

This common goal of the physical universe gives it a meaning and destination in the sacral order. But let us be on our guard in these matters, which are so easy to talk about but whose meaning is hidden. The religious finality of nature is not added to it as an extrinsic qualification. It must be said that nature itself, taken as such and in its specifically physical dynamism, is a ceaseless multiplication of the likeness of absolute being and goodness. Here, then, is the purpose of all things: *omnia intendunt assimilari Deo* (all things strive to be like God). They tend to this end of the movement itself with which they strive to conserve their being, which is an image of the pure act of being in which they share to the extent that they exist: *Secundum hoc autem esse habent omnia quod Deo assimilantur, qui est ipsum esse subsistens, cum omnia sint solum quasi esse participantia. Omnia igitur appetunt quasi ultimum finem Deo assimilari* (Now all things have their being from the fact that they resemble God, who is subsisting being itself, for all things are only as it were participants in being. Hence all things desire as their ultimate end to be made like God: *CG* 3.19.3). It is with a view to attaining this end that finite substances, which are not their own end, act, cause, and operate. Stretching language to its limit, St. Thomas describes the divine being as the substance itself of the existing God: *ipsum divinum esse est ipsius Dei existentis substantia* (*CG* 3.20.2). This is true of God alone. Because no created substance is its own being, it is not its own goodness. Hence it must acquire what it is not, and it can do this only by multiplying activities, aimed at completing the being and goodness that it is, while adding to them what they lack. Thus created substance tends to imitate God, not only imasmuch as it is, but also inasmuch as it acts in order to augment its own perfection: *non solum secundum esse substantiale, sed etiam ... secundum propriam operationem, quae etiam pertinet ad perfectionem rei* (not only according to its substantial being, but also ... according to its specific operation, which also belongs to the thing's perfection: *CG* 3.20.8).

This amounts to saying that physical causality itself is an imitation of the divine actuality. To cause is to tend to be like God: *res intendunt assimilari Deo in hoc quod sunt causae* (things tend to become like God inasmuch as they are causes: *CG* 3.21). Indeed we have just seen that created being tends to be like God from the simple fact that it acts, and because it cannot act without causing, it tends to be like God by the very fact that it causes its acts, but even more because it causes other beings. At this point the doctrine reveals its whole program: a God who is the pure act of being, to whom as such it is eminently fitting to be the cause of beings; and beings to which, as effects of this God, it is eminently appropriate in their turn to cause other beings. The Christian God is not a creator who creates creators, but he is a creator who creates efficient causes.

This is the source of all the difficulties accumulated by modern philosophies, and already by certain medieval philosophies and theologies, concerning the notion of efficient causality.

From St. Augustine and St. Bonaventure to Malebranche and his numerous school, we observe in many Christian masters a certain mistrust in this notion. There is no conception of efficacy that does not see in it, in some way, a causality of being. Now, is not the causing of the being of an effect dangerously like what it would be to create it? Hence the attenuations devised by certain philosophers and theologians to avoid ascribing to the creature the creator's own mode of causality. The "seminal principles" of Augustine and Bonaventure, the "occasional causes" of Malebranche, are so many doctrines intended to save the appearances of an efficient causality stripped of efficacy properly so called. Hume was not mistaken in this matter, and the skepticism with which he is charged – quite rightly, it must be added – testifies to a certain sense of mystery for him that is sometimes lacking in his opponents. In opposition to him, they are correct in maintaining the reality and the certainty of the relation of an efficient cause to its effect, but they are misguided if they hope to reduce it to a purely analytical relation of a principle to its conclusion. In a universe in which the prototype of causal efficacy is a creative act, the notion of efficient cause is enveloped in an aura of mystery; for while it itself is not a mystery, it is the analogue of the mysterious act between all things by which He Who Is has freely caused beings. The philosophical notion of efficient cause, understood as the power to produce a being, belongs by full right to Christian philosophy, precisely on the same ground and for the same reason as the notion of the act of being, for a cause is proportionate to being.[3] But today we know the sequence of events: theology produces metaphysics, then metaphysics prides itself in dispensing with the theology from which it comes; it soon becomes aware that it no longer understands itself; then philosophy takes up arms against metaphysics in the name of some kind of positivism or critique. What is most curious is the attitude adopted then by certain champions of metaphysics. In order the better to assure its survival, they set themselves up as defenders of its absolute independence. Especially concerned to protect it

3. [For the notion of efficient cause, see Gilson, *The Christian Philosophy of St. Thomas Aquinas*, pp. 178–184, and *Elements of Christian Philosophy* (Garden City, New York: Doubleday, 1960), pp. 184–202.]

from the inroads of theology, they are like persons who wanted to prevent a river from drying up while cutting it off from its source. The contrary must be done. The philosophical problems implicit in the metaphysical notion of efficient cause will never be well understood without relating it to the theological model that inspired it, namely the notion of creation.

Nothing is more evident in the doctrine of St. Thomas Aquinas, in which, for a being to be a cause is at the same time to make itself like God. Here the sacred character of a cause is as evident as that of being. "It is because of his goodness that God confers being on other things, for everything acts inasmuch as it is actually perfect. So all things desire to make themselves like God by becoming the cause of other things" (CG 3.21.3). In fact, the sign of the perfect actuality of a being is that it is able to produce other beings resembling it. So every being tends to perfect itself by striving to cause other beings, and thereby it tends to render itself similar to God (CG 3.21.6). Let us marvel again at the way this Christian philosophy is deepened as philosophy in proportion as it becomes more Christian, for there is nothing that a creature is or does that fails to resemble God; but the most excellent thing a creature does, after being, is to desire to be like God by causing other beings. As Dionysius says, "What is most divine is to become God's co-worker" (omnium divinius est Dei cooperatorem fieri).[4] Or, in the words of the Apostle, "We are God's fellow workers" (Dei sumus adjutores: 1 Cor. 3:9).

This is most true of us humans, who are the channels through which all things are directed to God. But it is also an absolutely general truth. For in fact everything, even natures devoid of knowledge, tend toward God by their activities. In a world created like this, the pursuit of particular ends coincides with that of the final end, and every being seeks beatitude while seeking its own well-being. We humans alone can know that we do it, but we would do it even if we were not conscious of doing it. This is what is meant by the "natural love" of God, which is disturbing only to those who have lost sight of what a created nature is, permeated

4. Dionysius the Pseudo-Areopagite, De coelesti hierarchia 3.2 [ed. Günter Heil, Corpus Dionysiacum 2, Patristische Texte und Studien 36 (Berlin and New York: Walter de Gruyter, 1991), pp. 17–19].

through and through and in all its acts with the divine efficacy that dwells within it, and in which it truly has being, movement, and life.

Compared to other doctrines, this one equally avoids a metaphysics of essences without existence and a metaphysics of existence without essences. It is in no way an existentialism in the latter sense. In it, every being is defined by its essence. Humanity is itself a nature whose freedom moves between the limits fixed by the terms of its definition: a living being whose specific mode of knowing is reasoning. The purpose of freedom is to assure the ever more perfect realization of the essence. To be a rational animal is not only a definition; it is a program. From birth to death every human being should work, in line with its individual capabilities, to become more and more what a knowing being should be, and always acting according to the light of reason. And not only for its own sake, but also for that of society, because it can fulfill the destiny which its nature as a knowing being imposes on it only in communion with other rational beings, who are seeking, like itself, to actualize themselves as perfectly as possible in the order of being and goodness. Existence is unfolded, then, from and within the essence, for the sake of realizing that same essence, but nevertheless on a field that is in a sense infinite, since over and above the particular end it wants to achieve, it is in fact directed to Him whose essence is being itself. To be a finite essence open to the pure act of being is something completely different from being an existence without purpose, a foolish freedom acting in a void. It is to be a being determined as a nature on the way to self-conquest, certain that no matter how far it advances in this life, its freedom will always be open to further progress.

We live in an age of the proliferation of cosmogonies, reasonable scientific fictions, but also captivating, as the works of the poetic imagination always are, even when it takes as its guide our provisional knowledge. These intelligible interpretations of the universe are so many romances of nature, in which the mind gives itself free rein to go beyond all conceivable verification of the limited certitudes of science. They are natural exercises of reason, and their results, which are very different from those obtained when the imagination starts with imaginary data, are very precious. Nevertheless, it is not to speak ill of these cosmogonies if we distinguish them from laws, or even from scientific theories experimentally verifiable within precise limits.

Metaphysics is no better qualified than science to relate the history of the universe, for it itself is not history. Centered on the knowledge of being as being, it can say what is, not how it has progressively become what it is. The panorama of creation can be interpreted in two different ways, and this can be done without altering any of its features. In both cases the universe appears as a hierarchy, the same hierarchy that is described in *Contra Gentiles* 3.1, where the pattern of nature is sketched according to the order of beings. First there is God, *perfectus in essendo et causando ... et in regendo* (perfect in being, causing, and governing); then intellectual creatures made to his image and likeness; then heavenly bodies, whose matter is incorruptible; then beings subject to generation and corruption; finally, prime matter (for it can be added to this list), concreated by God in the most lowly beings included in the created world.

The mind can traverse the stages of this hierarchy in two directions: from the top to the bottom, as Dionysius does in his writings, or from the bottom to the top, which is the natural procedure of the philosopher, ascending from effects to their cause, until the mind finally ends with the first uncaused cause. The most modern science does not question the reality of this hierarchical order in which, as Comte remarks, beings and the sciences treating of them are arranged according to an order of growing complexity and decreasing generality.[5] The only question is whether this tableau depicts a hierarchy given once and for all; or if, on the contrary, it describes the result of a slow evolution over millennia, which may or may not have been interrupted by sudden transformations (*révolutions*).[6]

5. [Auguste Comte, *Cours de philosophie positive*, 6 vols. (Paris: Schleicher Frères, 1908–1934), 1: 39. See Gilson's comments in *Recent Philosophy: Hegel to the Present*, by Etienne Gilson, Thomas Langan, and Armand Maurer, A History of Philosophy, ed. Gilson (New York: Random House, 1966), pp. 269–270, with p. 754 n6.]

6. [Raul Echauri is undoubtedly correct in interpreting Gilson to mean that, in the hypothesis of evolution, one of these "revolutions" would be the case of humankind descending from an animal, requiring divine intervention to bridge the immense distance between them. See his *El pensamiento de Etienne Gilson* (Pamplona: University of Navarra, S.A., 1980), p. 216. Gilson himself did not consider the transformation of species scientifically demonstrated: see his *From Aristotle to Darwin*

Metaphysics has no answer to this question, which belongs to "natural history" in the most exact sense of the term. Owing to its transcendence, theology is competent to judge all problems seen in a light analogous to that of the divine knowledge. It is remarkable that scripture has given an historical account of creation. Later, for example with St. Augustine, and undoubtedly influenced by the static quality of Greek metaphysics, it was thought right to consider the account of the six days of creation as a metaphorical description, designed for uneducated minds, of what was in fact the simple, instantaneous act by which God created everything at once: *creavit omnia simul* [Ecclus. 18:1]. Today, by a curious turnabout, what seemed the most satisfactory view of the universe not long ago has been replaced by another, dominated by the notion of evolution. However this term be understood, it means that today the order of beings is depicted as the result of a long history. We return, then, to the obvious literal, most simple, and quasi-popular sense of the account of Genesis; for it matters little whether the days are exactly six, or whether they are days of twenty-four hours or of x thousands of centuries. What matters is the fact that the present state of the world is the outcome of a history. Now, the metaphysician knows nothing about that. But the astronomer, the physicist, and the biologist think they know it; and, if it be true, it is scarcely a surprise to the theologian, for he always knew it. If there is an evolution of the universe, the theologian knows its origin, its supreme law, and its ending. Beginning with Him Who Is, under the infallible guidance of divine providence, and permeated from within by the efficacy of the pure act of being, the universe is directed to its ultimate goal, which is God. Philosophy is of very little use to theology on the subject of the final end of the world and the human race. Beyond the perspectives opened up by science and metaphysics, in this matter we must rely on the promises contained in the word of God.

These thoughts represent neither the theology of St. Thomas Aquinas nor his metaphysics, even less all the conclusions he held

---

and Back Again: A Journey in Final Causality, Species and Evolution, trans. John Lyon (Notre Dame, Ind.: University of Notre Dame Press, 1984), p. 89.]

as true in the area of the philosophy of nature. We have said nothing here about the human person, nothing about ethics or politics. But it was not our intention to speak of them. Our only wish was to elucidate as clearly as possible a small number of literally capital truths that must be grasped if the rest of the doctrine is to be understood.

All these truths depend on a certain notion of being, which was that of St. Thomas, and without which there is no Thomism truly worthy of the name. It is on this notion that we wanted to center attention. We have tried to clarify it by showing how certain other notions, like those of substance or cause, which are rightly accounted metaphysical principles, are tied up with it. We have not examined their applications in detail. Rather, we wanted to limit ourselves to throwing light on them, confident that, once the philosopher has grasped them, he need no longer fear to go wrong in applying them. True, their application is the work of a lifetime, but this work is a joy, especially if it is done under the guidance of a master like the Angelic Doctor and using a method like his own. By this we mean beginning with the same principles, understood in the sense in which he himself understood them, and in their light interpreting the universe of sensible experience as known to modern science.

Only those Christians will heed these words for whom theology, not metaphysics, remains wisdom *par excellence* and the only queen of the sciences truly worthy of the title. The whole future of Christian philosophy depends on an anticipated, willed, and hoped-for restoration of the true notion of theology that once flourished in the days of the great scholastic masters: William of Auvergne, Bonaventure, Albert the Great, Thomas Aquinas, John Duns Scotus, and the brilliant company of select minds who worked at the same task.[7] Those who fear that its restoration will mean the loss of metaphysics and science simply show that they are not aware of the authentic meaning of that notion. It is by losing their theology that they will lose their metaphysics. The

7. [In another context Gilson emphasizes the need for rejuvenating the "formulation" of theology in the light of modern discoveries in the physical and social sciences: see *The Philosopher and Theology*, trans. Cécile Gilson (New York: Random House, 1962), p. 217.]

misfortune of our time is that those who are most concerned about the indispensable restoration of *sacra doctrina* seem to be philosophers today who have neither authority nor competence to promote it.

Becoming a theologian requires preparation. Theology is only learned under a master, and fifty years of metaphysics are hardly enough to introduce the beginner to the meaning of the fundamentals of the doctrine.[8] But at least we ought to be able to make an appeal. Let us restore theology such as it was when it fulfilled the perfection of its essence, for Christian philosophy is doomed to die the moment it separates itself from it. Do not put Christian philosophers in the embarrassing position of having to defend this worthwhile object of their desire against some of those who have the vocation to preserve its heritage and from whom they would like to acquire it. As for knowing the attitude of non-Christian philosophers toward it, that is of little importance. For a long time metaphysics has been dying in their hands. Indeed, they have declared dead those of Plato and Aristotle, as well as that of St. Thomas Aquinas. As for those contemporaries who want to revive it, there is not one who does not theologize in his own way. Why would the only theology that openly appeals to the word of God also hesitate to speak out, not only among theologians but also among philosophers?

Perhaps they will turn a deaf ear to it; some at least are afraid of it. But that is not certain, and it is not even likely. The intellect has its own way of recognizing the truth. As soon as it hears it, and even before knowing why, it knows it to be true. This is because truth is the good of the intellect and because it loves it, however little it perceives of it, before plumbing its depths and really understanding it. What is more, we must make [the intellect] hear it, which we can always do if we wish, for that depends solely on us. And because, in the final analysis, it is not in our power to make the act effective, all God asks of us is that we make his word heard. What Christian would dare to refuse him this request?

8. [In his Aquinas Foundation Lecture, *Thomas Aquinas and Our Colleagues* (Princeton: Princeton University Press, 1953), Gilson argues that the study of metaphysics belongs to philosophical maturity.]

Index

accidents: their *esse* is *inesse* 121

agent intellect: as light of intellect 70–72

Albert the Great, St. 133

Anaxagoras: intellect, 18, 52

Anselm, St. 10, 62

Aristotle: xvii, 11, 12, 14, 15, 19, 20, 22, 23, 45, 51, 52, 77, 106; essences are like numbers 116; essential form is most formal constitutive of being 122; God is the cause of all being and truth 96; intellect 71, 72; no creation *ex nihilo* 95; principles 73

Augustine, St. ix, xiv; days of creation 132; divine begetting 82; divine ideas 103, 104, 107–109; God's immutable being: *see* God; and Platonism 70, 72; seminal principles 128; senses of scripture 19, 27

Averroes 12, 19, 64; Averroists 15

Avicenna 11, 12, 19, 64, 94; essence and existence 57, 58; necessary and possible being 59 n7; proof of God's existence 21; proof of necessary being 60; substance 121

Bañez, Domingo: causation of *esse* 93 n3; *esse* "imperfected" by essence 117; *esse* means existence 120

Bartholomew of Capua 78 n2

being: act and potency, as modes of 123, 124; arguments for a cause of universal being 19–21; idolatrous concept, according to Marion xxiii; not representable 102; object of metaphysics xxiv, 67, 68, 73, 74; origin of the notion 84, 85; stages in quest of universal cause of 16–19. *See also ens; esse;* essence; existence; substance

Boethius 46

Bonaventure, St. ix, xiv, 133; divine illumination 69, 70; exemplarism 108; seminal principles 128

cause: arguments for a cause of universal being 19–21; efficient 127–129; of the *esse* of things; primary and instrumental 93

Christian philosophy: and *Aeterni Patris* xiii, 3; criticism of ix, x, 64, 65; deepens philosophy and aids theology 32; future of depends on restoration of scholastic theology 133; ideal form was that practiced by medieval theologians xx, 133; rational yet developed within faith and theology xvi–xx, 28;

relation to faith and theology 32; a way of philosophizing rather than a doctrine xiii, xiv. *See also* being; Gilson, Etienne; God; metaphysics; philosophy; Scholastics: scholastic philosophy; theology; Thomism

Comte, Auguste xix; order of universal knowledge 131; religion of positivism 67

Damascene, John, St. 45, 62; God as infinite ocean of entity 41

Descartes, René xviii, 10, 67; attitude to existence 74

Dionysius, the Pseudo-Areopagite: cooperating with God 129; hierarchy of creation 131; negative theology 43

Duns Scotus: *see* Scotus

Echauri, Raul: Gilson on evolution 131 n6

Empedocles 18

ens: a being, that which is (*habens esse*) xx, xxi, 34, 60, 86, 116, 120. *See also* being

esse: act of being or existing xx, xxi, 34, 60, 102, 120; actuality of form and nature 29, 125; and individuality 54; fixed and at rest in a being 122; more formal than essence 122; proper effect of God 91, 92, 97; proofs of real composition of and essence in creatures presuppose notion of God as pure act of being xxi, xxii, 31; real distinction between *esse* and essence in fi-

nite beings 29–31, 34, 56–64; supreme actuality and perfection xxi, 116–118; two meanings: act of being or the composition of a proposition 37. *See also* being

essence: importance of 55; a limitation of *esse* 34; modality of being 115–117; potential to *esse* 118; praise of 118; a scattering of being 103. *See also* being

existence (*existentia*): and *esse* 120. *See also* being

Fichte, Johann 56

Francis of Assisi, St. 39

Gilson, Etienne: idea of Christian philosophy: *see* Christian philosophy; *Introduction à la philosophie chrétienne* (*Christian Philosophy: An Introduction*), its composition and purpose xi–xii; on evolution xx n41, 131, 132; on philologists xxii, 25, 26; his deepening understanding of theology and its relation to Christian philosophy xiv–xvi; writings on Christian philosophy ix–x

Gioberti, Vincenzo and ontologism 84 n5

God: absolute transcendence of 86; affirmative and negative knowledge of 35, 43, 44; beyond being (*ens*) 33, 34, 98; cannot be represented xxiv, 84; embraced only by love 39, 86; his *esse* unknown 38, 40, 86; his essence and *esse* are